THE IDEAS COMPANION

Johnny Acton

A THINK BOOK FOR

ROBSON BOOKS

*Ideas are meant to be copied.
I prefer that they are stolen so that I don't
have to use them myself*

Salvador Dali

THINK
A Think Book
for Robson Books

First published in Great Britain in 2005 by
Robson Books
151 Freston Road, London W10 6TH

An imprint of Anova Books Company Ltd

Edited by Johnny Acton
The Companion team: Tilly Boulter, James Collins, Rhiannon Guy,
Emma Jones, Jo Swinnerton, Lou Millward Tait and Malcolm Tait
Cover illustration: John See

Think Publishing
The Pall Mall Deposit
124-128 Barlby Road, London W10 6BL
www.thinkpublishing.co.uk

Computer Patent Annuities Limited Partnership
CPA House, 11-15 Seaton Place
St Helier, Jersey JE1 1BL, Channel Islands
www.cpaglobal.com

ISBN 1-86105-835-7

Printed and bound in Italy by ▓▓ Grafica Veneta S.p.A.

*I have not failed. I've just found
ten thousand ways that won't work*

Thomas Alva Edison

WITH THANKS

Many people have helped me with this book, but the following deserve special thanks:

Maria Parker, for making this book a reality.

Chris Martin for the initial introduction.

Bianca, Charlotte, Helen, Micky and all at CPA for their enthusiasm, ideas and feedback.

Vicky Bamforth, Nicola Haynes, Lois Lee, James Molony, Vincent Powell and Nancy Waters for ideas and research.

Joel Barry for providing a lawyer's perspective.

Patricia Acton, Adam Sutcliffe, Chris Thirsk, Pam Robertson and Ajax Scott for allowing the editor to pick their professional brains.

Lai Yap and Jason Priestly for their linguistic expertise.

Nick Sandler for morale-boosting games of table tennis.

As ever, my wife.

INTRODUCTION

The world we live in has been shaped by ideas and inventions. The urge to innovate is a fundamental characteristic of our species. Unless we happen to be in a desert or on the polar ice-cap (in which case we almost certainly relied on human ingenuity to get us there), the evidence is all around us.

Like many of us, I have long been fascinated by inventors and their creations, from the first balloonists to the discovery of Silly Putty. There are intriguing and inspiring stories behind 'eureka' moments great and small. But equally fascinating – and increasingly important – are the measures individuals and organisations have taken to claim ownership of new ideas. Or sometimes to subvert the process.

Twenty years ago, few people had heard the phrase 'intellectual property' (IP). Today, you can't get away from it. We are literally surrounded by legally protected material, from songs and literature to household items bristling with design and utility patents. Our CDs and DVDs bear dire warnings of the legal consequences of unauthorised use. Celebrities milk their image rights for all they are worth. And the average Westerner comes across 1,500 trademarks every day, a figure rising twenty-fold if he or she ventures into a supermarket. That's one for every day of an 80-year lifespan. On the legal side, the scope of the IP industry is widening all the time – smells, colours and even living organisms are now considered fair game. And society is becoming ever more litigious. If ever there was a growth industry, it's IP.

This book is a pan-optic survey of that weird and wonderful world. It makes no pretence of being an exhaustive guide to the subject. Instead, it works on the principle of 'organised chaos', seeking to give a holistic view by providing a little bit of everything. From Neolithic trademarks to the movie star who invented the radio-controlled torpedo, from absurd copyright squabbles to moments of divine inspiration, if it's IP related it's here. Quite what you make of it is up to you. One thing's for sure: you won't get an education like this from a textbook…

Author's Note

This book has been a joy to write, but knowing that a high percentage of readers are likely to be lawyers, it has also been slightly terrifying. I have tried to be scrupulously balanced and legally sound while remaining true to the (occasionally irreverent) spirit of the Companion series. The book has to be a bit risqué sometimes to do the job properly. So please be kind – I'm only a little guy.

Johnny Acton

Celebration, Florida is a town developed by The Walt Disney Company to enshrine the corporation's good old-fashioned American values. Founded in 1994, Celebration was built on land owned by Disney, and previously used to relocate alligators that strayed too close to guest quarters at the adjacent Disney World.

The town was designed in line with the philosophy of 'new urbanism', with a strategic blending of parks and residential and commercial space. Celebration's bank, post office, cinema and town hall were all designed by big-name architects. Residents glide by on Segway scooters or in small electric 'NEVs' (Neighborhood Electric Vehicles). The emphasis is on community, with planned events throughout the year. At Christmas, for example, 'snow' (actually foam) is blown onto Market Street by discreet machines mounted on lamp-posts.

Celebration is a genuine town. It is not gated, for example, and both commercial and residential properties are traded in a regular, if heavily regulated way. But the town is unusual in having a registered trademark for a seal.

Celebration is said to strongly resemble Seaside, also in Florida, the town used to represent the central character's too-good-to-be-true home in the film *The Truman Show*. And British techno-punks Chumbawamba recorded a none-too kind song about Celebration on their album *WYS/WYG* (2000).

USELESS PATENTS

The 'Spider Ladder'

GB patent no. 2,272,154 does just what it says on the tin. It's a spider-sized ladder that helps spiders to clamber up the side of a bath. Held in place by a suction pad, the 'spider ladder' offers our eight-legged friends the perfect escape from a watery grave.

LIBERTY X

Sometimes losing can work in your favour, as designer pop outfit Liberty X have managed to prove twice. Formed in 2001 by the five losers of the final heat of the UK version of the 'Find-a-band' TV show *Popstars*, Liberty X have gone on to eclipse the winners of the competition (Hear'Say) in both sales and popularity. Originally X-less, they have also benefited greatly from losing an intellectual property case in which an obscure 70s band successfully challenged their right to the name 'Liberty'. The enforced addition of the 24th letter of the alphabet suddenly made them sexy.

10 *Years in succession IBM had been awarded more US patents than any other company as of 2002*

THE CREATION OF FUTUREMOUSE

Magid is assistant to Marcus Chalfen, a biologist intent on perfecting the human race. FutureMouse, whose birth is described below, is a crucial step in his programme. The rodent has been genetically engineered to live for nine years, and Chalfen is anxious to patent the process.

Magid was proud to say he witnessed every stage. He witnessed the custom design of the genes. He witnessed the germ injection. He witnessed the artificial insemination. And he witnessed the birth, so different from his own. One mouse only. No battle down the birth canal, no first and second, no saved and unsaved. No pot-luck. No random factors. No *you have your father's snout and your mother's love of cheese.* No mysteries lying in wait. No doubt as to when death will arrive. No hiding from illness, no running from pain. No question about who was pulling the strings. No doubtful omnipotence. No shaky fate. No question of a journey, no question of greener grass, for wherever this mouse went, its life would probably be the same. It would not travel through time... because its future was equal to its present which was equal to its past. A Chinese box of a mouse. No other roads, no missed opportunities, no parallel possibilities. No second-guessing, no what-ifs, no might-have-beens. Just certainty. Just certainty in its purest form. And what's more, thought Magid – once the witnessing was over, once the mask and gloves were removed, once the white coat was returned to its hook – what is more God than that?

Zadie Smith, *White Teeth*

ACCIDENTAL INVENTIONS

Cellophane

In 1900, Jacques E Brandenberger witnessed an anonymous Swiss diner spill red wine over a restaurant tablecloth. The cloth ruined, Brandenberger decided then and there to do something about it. But inventing a clear flexible film that could provide a waterproof layer for tablecloths was not as easy as he had expected. His experiments seemed only to render the cloth stiff, not waterproof. Down but not out, Brandenberger noticed that the coating on his latest attempt peeled off as a transparent film, and, quick to realise that this was not a useless by-product but the start of something big, he set about developing a machine for the mass manufacture of what we know today as 'cellophane'. By 1908, Brandenberger had patented his invention and his machine. Today, cellophane finds use in food packaging, but is also the base for self-adhesive tapes such as Sellotape.

For the first time in his life, Tim began to doubt his father's advice: 'No point in reinventing the wheel'.

DREADFUL ADVICE

While working on his 1999 album 2001, rap artist Dr Dre sought advice from a prominent musicologist about his plan to use a five note bass-line from Fatback's 1980 R&B hit *Backstrokin'* on a track called entitled *Let's Get High*. The musicologist advised him that the sequence was 'commonplace'. Two years later, Minder Music, owners of the copyright for *Backstrokin'*, successfully sued Dre for $1.5 million.

COCA-COLA SLOGANS: THE FIRST 60 YEARS

1886	Drink Coca-Cola
1904	Delicious and Refreshing
1905	Coca-Cola Revives and Sustains
1906	The Great National Temperance Beverage
1917	Three Million a Day
1922	Thirst Knows No Season
1923	Enjoy Thirst
1924	Refresh Yourself
1925	Six Million a Day
1926	It Had to Be Good to Get Where It Is
1927	Pure as Sunlight
1927	Around the Corner from Everywhere
1929	The Pause that Refreshes
1932	Ice Cold Sunshine
1938	The Best Friend Thirst Ever Had
1939	Whoever You Are, Wherever You May Be, When You Think of Refreshment Think of Coca-Cola
1942	The Only Thing Like Coca-Cola Is Coca-Cola Itself

QUOTE UNQUOTE

Innovation makes enemies of all those who prospered under the old regime, and only lukewarm support is forthcoming for those who would prosper under the new. Their support is indifferent partly from fear and partly because they are generally incredulous, never really trusting new things until they have tested them by experience.
Niccolo Machiavelli, Italian politician and author

PATENTING CURRY

Although people tend to associate curry with India, in 1999 two Japanese businessmen (Hirayama Makoto and Ohashi Sachiyo) lodged a patent application audaciously claiming that they had invented the dish. The patent application was made by House Foods Corp, one of Japan's top food and drink companies. 'The cooking of curry is carried out by mixing ingredients such as onion, potato, carrot and meat...with water...[and] extract of turmeric, cumin and coriander', the document read, 'heating over a slow fire for 10–20 minutes after boiling, adding wheat flour roux and curry powder or adding curry roux and heating until the mixture becomes viscous.'

The curry application was relatively straightforward in comparison with some cases. Since it became apparent that the Patent Office was prepared to endorse culinary borrowing of this kind, more than 80 Japanese firms have since claimed to have invented pizza.

THE 8 MOST DOWNLOADED PROJECT GUTENBERG BOOKS

Project Gutenberg is a US-hosted website from which entire books may be downloaded by the public. The site notes that the 12,000 titles in its archives are either in the public domain in the US or made available for free distribution by permission of the authors, but advises readers outside of the US to take note of national copyright laws. Its stated aim is 'To encourage the creation and distribution of eBooks.'

The eBooks available range from the Notebooks of Leonardo da Vinci and Gibbon's *History of the Decline and Fall of the Roman Empire* to lesser-known works such as William Sangster's *Umbrellas and their History* or Lilian C McNamara Garis's *Girl Scout Pioneers*.

**At the time of writing the top eight eBooks
accessed from the site were:**

1. *Hand Shadows to Be Thrown upon the Wall,* Henry Bursill
2. *The Complete Notebooks of Leonardo Da Vinci,*
   Leonardo da Vinci
3. *The Art of War,* Sun Zi
4. *Ulysses,* James Joyce
5. *How to Speak and Write Correctly,* Joseph Devlin
6. *Relativity: the Special and General Theory*, Albert Einstein
7. *Grimm's Fairy Tales*, Jacob and Wilhelm Grimm
8. *The Koran (Al-Qur'an)*

BRAND HOPPING

Get from 'SONY' to 'COKE' in four steps, changing one letter each time. Each of the three intervening words has to make sense.
Answer on page 153.

CELEBRITY INVENTORS

Jamie Lee Curtis

In 1988, US Patent No. 4,753,647 was issued to the actress Jamie Lee Curtis, of *Trading Places* and *Fish Called Wanda* fame.

The Dipe 'N' Wipe has a moisture-proof pocket on the front containing wipes that can be taken out and applied with one hand, a big advantage when you're trying to hold a baby. But JLC (now Lady Haden-Guest) has refused to allow her invention to be mass-produced until chemists start selling biodegradable nappies.

THE GRANDCHILDREN CAN
TAKE CARE OF THEMSELVES

Mark Twain (Samuel L Clemens) was a passionate proponent of copyright legislation, at least towards the end of his life. When, in 1883, the editor of the *Boston Musical Record* wrote to solicit his opinion on a proposed international copyright treaty, he could not summon up much enthusiasm. 'I am 47 years old,' Twain replied, 'and therefore shall not live long enough to see international copyright established; neither will my children live long enough; yet, for the sake of my (possible) remote descendants, I feel a languid interest in the subject.' But his attitude had stiffened considerably by the time he appeared before a Washington committee 23 years later. The proposal under consideration was the extension of the period of an author's copyright from 42 years outright to 50 years after the date of his or her demise:

'I have read this bill. At least I have read such portions as I could understand. Nobody but a practised legislator can read the bill and thoroughly understand it, and I am not a practised legislator. I am interested particularly and especially in the part of the bill which concerns my trade. I like that extension of copyright life to the author's life and fifty years afterward. I think that would satisfy any reasonable author, because it would take care of his children. Let the grand-children take care of themselves. That would take care of my

daughters, and after that I am not particular. I shall then have long been out of this struggle, independent of it, indifferent to it.

It isn't objectionable to me that all the trades and professions in the United States are protected by the bill. I like that. They are all important and worthy, and if we can take care of them under the copyright law I should like to see it done. I should like to see oyster culture added, and anything else.

I am aware that copyright must have a limit, because that is required by the Constitution of the United States, which sets aside the earlier Constitution, which we call the decalogue. The decalogue says you shall not take away from any man his profit. I don't like to be obliged to use the harsh term. What the decalogue really says is, "Thou shalt not steal", but I am trying to use more polite language. The laws of England and America do take it away, do select but one class, the people who create the literature of the land. They always talk handsomely about the literature of the land, always what a fine, great, monumental thing a great literature is, and in the midst of their enthusiasm they turn around and do what they can to discourage it. I know we must have a limit, but forty-two years is too much of a limit. I am quite unable to guess why there should be a limit at all to the possession of the product of a man's labor. There is no limit to real estate.'

THE WORLD'S FIRST PAYPHONE

The coin-operated telephone was patented by William Gray of Hartford, Connecticut. The first model was installed in the Hartford Bank in 1889. Soon the devices were cropping up in hotels, bars, restaurants and shops.

John Paul Getty, then one of the richest men in the world, installed a pay-phone for the use of his guests at his mansion in England.

THOUGHTS FROM THE AUTHOR OF THE HUNCHBACK OF NOTRE DAME

Before the publication, the author has an undeniable and unlimited right. Think of a man like Dante, Molière, Shakespeare. Imagine him at the time when he has just finished a great work. His manuscript is there, in front of him; suppose that he gets the idea to throw it into the fire; nobody can stop him. Shakespeare can destroy Hamlet, Molière Tartufe, Dante the Hell. But as soon as the work is published, the author is not any more the master. It is then that other persons seize it; call them what you will: human spirit, public domain, society.

Victor Hugo, when chair of l'Association Littéraire Internationale during the 1870s

THE BRILLIANT MR BRILLIANT

Ashleigh Brilliant is a full-time epigram writer. He has copyrighted 5,632 one-liners, and obtained damages for their unlicensed use from everyone from Funny Side Up (which produced underpants bearing the legend 'I may not be perfect but parts of me are excellent') to 3M (which gave its staff Post-its printed with Brilliant slogan 212: 'All I want is a little more than I'll ever get'). His wife estimates that his work has featured on 100 million items and brings in about US$100,000 per annum, about half coming from greetings card. But he will occasionally allow somebody to use his material for free. Joe A Fear of Leadville, Colorado asked for permission to carve thought No. 1041 on his wife's gravestone. Mr Brilliant acceded, but with one condition: the stone had to be inscribed with his full name and the copyright symbol. 'These could be in quite small lettering and in an inconspicuous position', he told Mr Fear, who was happy to comply. Mrs Fear's gravestone (in the Mount Olivet Cemetery in Buena Vista, Colorado) now reads: 'Frances G Fear. Before I knew the best part of my life had come, it had gone. ©Ashleigh Brilliant'

INTELLECTUAL PROPERTY PARADOXES

When, in June 2000, a US federal court ordered software giant Microsoft to be split up, there was outrage among people concerned about anti-trust abuse. John Berthoud, president of the 300,000-member National Taxpayers Union, accused the authorities of 'seeking the ultimate legal paradox – a precedent without precedence. They've claimed that Microsoft is a monopoly without establishing a motive... [and] sought to share the firm's intellectual property without showing how it will help promote private enterprise.'

'Unless taxpayers convince Congress', Mr Berthoud continued, 'to act against break-up schemes and intellectual property thefts that masquerade under the rule of law, our economic freedoms will never be secure from this government.'

QUOTE UNQUOTE

'Therefore, behold, I am against the prophets', saith the LORD,
'that steal my words every one from his neighbour.'
Jeremiah 23:30

TOP 20 COMPANIES BY US PATENTS
RECEIVED 1999–2003

IBM	15,756
Canon	9,447
NEC	8,818
Micron	7,420
Samsung	7,077
Matsushita	6,947
Sony	6,903
Hitachi	6,809
Fujitsu	6,018
Toshiba	5,895
Mitsubishi	5,864
GE	5,148
AMD	5,022
Intel	5,006
Lucent	4,955
Philips	4,578
Motorola	4,488
Hewlett-Packard	4,193
Eastman Kodak	4,028
Siemens	3,761

Source: United States Patent and Trademark Office

US patent number of T Blanchard's circular sawing machine of 1836 17

ACCIDENTAL INVENTIONS

Velcro

Often erroneously believed to have been developed as part of the American Space programme, Velcro was actually invented in 1948 by a Swiss engineer who had just been walking his dog. When George de Mestral got home, he noticed that both he and his pet were covered in burrs (the seed-sacs of plants that typically spread themselves by hitching rides on the fur of passing animals). Suddenly an idea struck him. Ignoring the dog, he plucked one of the offending items from his cloth jacket and raced to his microscope. Under magnification, the infuriating secret of the burr was revealed. It was covered with hooked strands, and these, he realised, would inevitably cling to the coat of a beast that rubbed up against it. In the case of his jacket, Mistral reasoned that the hooks formed an even firmer bond by slotting into tiny loops in the fabric.

Mistral knew at once that the burr principle could be used to develop a revolutionary fastening device, but it took him several years to perfect his invention. The main difficulty was getting the 'loop' side of the fastener right (the 'hook' side was more straightforward). The solution turned out to be to sew the loops from nylon under infra-red light.

In 1951, Mistral applied for a Swiss patent for an early version of his fastening system. He christened it 'Velcro' (the word is a combination of 'crochet' and 'velour') and opened his first factory the following year. In 1955, he obtained a US patent for his invention, and two years later Velcro went into production in Manchester, New Hampshire. Before long, the company was selling 60 million yards per annum. Looking at plants can pay.

BRIAN LARA

In June 1994, the West Indian cricketer Brian Lara made a world-record 501-not-out for Warwickshire against Durham. This caused consternation in the jeans world. Lara had a sponsorship deal with Joe Bloggs Jeans, but had inadvertently given a great boost to a rival company by publicising the number associated with its most famous product (Levi's 501). Neither manufacturer was exactly delighted. Bloggs couldn't bring out a '501' jean and Levi Strauss couldn't sign up the player to exploit his achievement. Lara's agents were left to rue the fact that their client hadn't scored one run more or fewer – the marketing possibilities would have been endless. Fortunately, Lara had made a test record 375 for the West Indies against England two months earlier and would go onto break it with a score of 400 just 10 years later, so he still provided them with commercially valuable numbers.

18 *Percentage of voters choosing the wheel as the greatest human invention in a 2004 survey by scenta.co.uk.*

IP TERMS REDEFINED

Monopol(l)y

QUOTE UNQUOTE

It's much too good for him. He didn't know what to do with it!
George Frideric Handel, when asked why he had borrowed music
from the composer Giovanni Maria Bononcini

3 MOVIES WITH AN IP-ISH THEME

The Man in the White Suit
(1951) – Boffin Alec Guinness
threatens the future of manufacturing by inventing an indestruc-
tible material.

The Water Engine (1992) – An
inventor comes up with the solution to human energy needs but
encounters ruthless opposition
from vested business interests.

Men in Black (1997) – Will
Smith and Tommy Lee Jones are
alien-chasers, working for a
secretive and immensely
wealthy NGO. The organisation gets its money from patents
for microwave ovens, Velcro
and liposuction machines,
which Jones reveals were confis-
cated from extraterrestrial
invaders.

US plant patent number for a coral red dahlia 'shading to Eugenia red towards 19
the center' (1932)

IBSEN THE LUDDITE

I'm afraid for all those who'll have the bread snatched from their mouths by these machines. What business has science and capitalism got, bringing all these new inventions into the works, before society has produced a generation educated up to using them?

Henrik Ibsen

MOTHERS, DAUGHTERS AND SISTERS OF INVENTION

Josephine Cochran invented a dishwasher in 1886, sold her machines in restaurants in Chicago and set up the Garis Cochran Dishwasher Company.

Mary Anderson invented a highly practical windscreen wiper after a visit to New York in 1903 when she watched amazed as the tram drivers got out of their cabs to wipe snow from the windscreen.

Barbara Askins developed a new way of enhancing photographs using radioactive materials for NASA bringing pictures into focus for the first time. This technology was also used to improve x-ray technology and she was the first woman to be named National Inventor of the Year in 1978.

SPAM BY NUMBERS

1937 Year that the tinned meat made its appearance in the US.

$100 Prize given to the person who came up with the name spam in a competition. It was originally called 'Hormel Spiced Ham'.

4 Number of cans of spam, on average, that every resident of Hawaii eats per year. Hawaiians are the world's biggest spam consumers.

500,000 Number of spamburgers served each year on each of the three spammobiles, the spam-shaped lorries that promote spam throughout the US.

Source: www.spam.com

NON-FREEDOM OF EXPRESSION

In 1998, the writer Kembrew McLeod successfully registered the phrase 'freedom of expression' with the United States Patent and Trademark Office, under class 16 of the International Schedule. This covers printed matter. Writers are therefore no longer free to use the expression without McLeod's consent. Fortunately, he was being ironic (unless we get a letter to the contrary).

20 *Percentage of working week Google.com allows its employees to devote to their own projects*

WORD PUZZLE

What nefarious activity is concealed below?
NPIRAECYT
Answer on page 153.

WHO'S THE DADDY? YOU DECIDE

COCA-COLA		PEPSI-COLA
John Pemberton, pharmacist, brewed up first batch in a brass kettle in 1886	**Founding father**	Caleb Bradham, pharmacist, offered drink to customers at his soda fountain in 1898
31 January 1893	**Trademark granted**	16 June 1903
Orange-based, more fizz	**What's the difference?**	Lemon-based, sweeter, flatter
'Dynamic Ribbon' or Coke Wave' introduced in 1970	**Familiar face**	Pepsi 'Globe'
'Contour Bottle' developed to foil copycats in 1915	**Shape**	'Swirl' bottle introduced in 1958
First slogan: Delicious! Refreshing! Invigorating!	**Sound familiar?**	First slogan: Exhilarating, invigorating, aids digestion
Red and White	**Colour mode**	Red, white and blue
'New Coke' alienates consumers in 1985. Original recipe quickly reinstated.	**Biggest mistake**	Bradham gambles on the sugar prices on the stock market and bankrupts company in 1923. Assets sold for US$30,000.
Vanilla Coke	**Hope for the future**	Pepsi Blue
US$69 billion; ranked 1st in the world*	**Brand value**	US$6 billion (44th)*

Source: Interbrand

1790 The year Samuel Hopkins was granted the first US patent – for 'making pot and pearl ashes', a cleaning formula used in the soap making process.

4 million The sum, in pounds, of damages awarded to Dyson for infringement of its dual cyclone patent by Hoover. According to Dyson, it would have settled for one million pounds if the case had not gone to the high court.

618–907 The years of the Tang Dynasty, during which the militia monks of Shaolin earned their notoriety. They are now seeking to protect the Shaolin name, widely used on products unlicensed by the monastery.

344,717 The record number of applications received by the US Patent and Trademark Office in 2001. The European Patent Office fielded 158,200 filings in 2001, with electronic communications, medical technology and electrical components the most prolific sectors.

100 million The estimated worth, in dollars, of 'auction patents' that are the subject of dispute between eBay and Virginia inventor Tom Woolston.

3,454 The number of US patents issued to IBM during 2001. Once again, leading the pack in innovation.

22 Average number of months it takes to receive a US patent.

Sources: AP, BBC, EPO, IBM, USPTO

QUOTE UNQUOTE

A word beginning with 'X'… the more we thought about it, the more we were ready to try it. And we got it into the dictionary.
John B Hartnett, former Chairman of Xerox Corp,
on the origin of the company's trademark.

PRODUCTS DENIED TO THE WORLD

In 1983, the comedian Johnny Carson invoked the Right of Publicity to prevent the sale of 'Here's Johnny Portable Toilets'. Although the product featured neither the name nor likeness of the litigant, a Michigan court ruled that it might as well have done, so strong was the association in the public mind between Mr Carson and the phrase used to introduce him on *The Tonight Show*. Entrepreneurs tempted to manufacture a 'Shut that door!' draught excluder should take heed.

22 *Average daily number of design and plant patents awarded to residents of New York State in 2000*

IN PRAISE OF THE WRIGHT BROTHERS

Of all the inventions that have helped to unify China perhaps the aeroplane is the most outstanding. Its ability to annihilate distance has been in direct proportion to its achievements in assisting to annihilate suspicion and misunderstanding among provincial officials far removed from one another or from the officials at the seat of government.

> **Madame Chiang Kai-Shek, Chinese politician and wife of former Nationalist leader, quoted in the *Shang-hai Evening Post*, 12 March 1937**

FOOTBALLERS AND INTELLECTUAL PROPERTY

Soccer fans who purchased the computer game FIFA 2002 were amazed to find lovable goalkeeper Oliver Kahn omitted from the virtual Bayern Munich and Germany team line-ups. It transpired that Mr Kahn did not belong to any of the players' organisations that had licensed Electronic Arts to use their members' names and images.

FAMOUS PEOPLE WHO WORKED IN A PATENT OFFICE

- Albert Einstein (in Berne, Switzerland)
- Arthur Pedrick (British inventor)
- Chester F Carlesen (inventor of the modern photocopier)
- AE Housman (English poet, author of *A Shropshire Lad*)
- Clara Barton (first president of the American Red Cross)

SAY IT WITH CIGARETTES

According to the Beijing Famous Brand Estimate Company Limited, the most valuable brand in China as of 2001 was the Hongtashan low tar cigarette. Its value was estimated at 46 billion yuan, then equivalent to US$5.56 billion. This came as a surprise to some analysts, who noted that a packet of Hongtashan, at 14 yuan, cost almost as much as the average non-skilled worker earned in a day (15 Yuan). Using minimum wages as a guide, this equates to around $45 in the USA and £37 in the UK. It transpired that the cigarettes tended to be purchased as gifts or baksheesh, sure to go down well in a country with 300 million committed smokers.

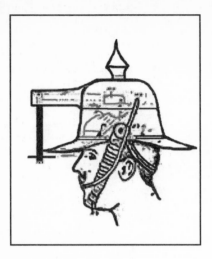

Had James Bond's gadget-maker Q been alive in the days when soldiers still wore spikes on their helmets, he might have come up with something on the lines of this ingenious helmet-rifle. In any event, he was beaten to it by a man named Pratt. But Pratt's invention was not entirely successful – the recoil from the device broke a man's neck during early trials.

QUOTE UNQUOTE

This is a restaurant, not a song.
Dallas businessman Bill Arnold in 2000. Rock band 'The Eagles' had filed suit against him for naming his 'Hotel California Grill' after their hit 1976 song *Hotel California*.

THE CHINESE GOT THERE FIRST

Although Europeans might assume that the world's first laws to regulate publishing were made in their own continent, they'd be wrong. The reason is simple: printing was established in China a thousand years before it hit the West. In 835, the emperor Wen-Tsing issued an ordinance forbidding the private printing of almanacs.

LANDMARKS IN THE HISTORY
OF GENETIC PATENTS

In 1984, Harvard professor Philip Leder and Timothy Stewart, then of the University of California, unveiled the Oncomouse, a rodent genetically engineered to develop cancer. The purpose of this was to facilitate the development of new drugs to combat the disease. Four years later, the United States Patent and Trademark Office granted patents on the oncomouse, its offspring and the relevant engineering process.

BRANDS AND BANDS

Half way into 2004, Agenda Inc, a San Francisco marketing firm, reported on the use of brand-names in the lyrics of Billboard Top 20 songs over the previous six months. The company noted that there had been 645 instances in the year to date compared with 643 in the same period in 2003. Brands benefiting from the most references were Cadillac (41 mentions), with Hennessy in second place on 39 and Gucci and Rolls Royce tying for third with 26 each. There were also first appearances for Geico and the Bank of America.

IP UNDER COMMUNISM

The Intellectual Property law of the old Soviet Union was based on the principle that the role of artists and authors was to enshrine the life and ideas of a socialist society. The publication and dissemination of works was exclusively controlled by the state, and no copyright fees were payable for works broadcast through the mass media. But other public performances were subject to compulsory licences, and these gave authors the right to equitable remuneration.

ACCIDENTAL INVENTIONS

Modern Fingerprinting

Although the science of fingerprinting began with the work of Francis Galton in the nineteenth century, detectives still had trouble locating the tell-tale marks. Then, in 1982, some researchers at the US Army Criminal Investigation Laboratory in Japan cracked a fish tank. When they patched it together with superglue (cyanoacrylate), they noticed the fingerprints on the glass standing out in proud relief. The fumes from the glue had condensed on oils in the prints, rendering them highly visible. Cyanoacrylate is now an important weapon in the forensic scientist's armoury.

Sum, in millions of Kenyan Shillings, that Microskills Ltd was ordered to pay 25
Microsoft after being found guilty of software piracy in 2000

...obtained Jan 1977 to June 2000

1. Nike
2. Black & Decker
3. Rubbermaid
4. Motorola
5. Goodyear Tire and Rubber Company
6. Dart Industries
7. IBM

ACCIDENTAL INVENTIONS

The Post-It

There may be several years between an invention and the moment of inspiration when someone finally works out what to do with it.

In 1968, 3M research scientist Dr Spence Silver was working on a project to improve the glue used for the company's various adhesive tapes. One day, he came up with a substance that was useless for the job at hand but nonetheless had several interesting properties. It formed itself into tiny spheres that were remarkably durable (which wouldn't melt or dissolve) and extremely sticky individually. But if a tape was coated with the substance and applied to a surface, only a small proportion of the spheres would adhere. In other words, you could use the tape again and again but it was lousy at holding things together.

For the next five years, Silver touted his invention around the company, squirting out samples from a spray-can. His colleagues were impressed, but couldn't see much future in an unsticky glue. Then in 1973, a new product development manager named Geoff Nicholson joined 3M's Commercial Tape division and became fascinated by Silver's strange adhesive. He started to investigate ways of using it for posting messages on bulletin-boards. But the real moment of inspiration took place in church. Art Fry, a 3M product development researcher who had grown up in Iowa, was driven to distraction by the bookmark repeatedly falling out of his hymn book while he was trying to sing in the choir. Suddenly he remembered Silver's strange substance from work. It would be perfect for bookmarks! And thus the Post-It was born.

'You can't predict it', Fry later said of the moment when everything clicked, 'but you can do the work that will lead you to those things.'

IN THE PINK

In 1987, Owens Corning was granted a trademark for a particular shade of pink used to distinguish its insulation products.

PRODUCTS DENIED TO THE WORLD

In 1989, Balducci Publications printed an advertisement for a fictitious product named 'Michelob Oily' on the back of its *Snicker* magazine. The central motif was a fish being doused with oil from a receptacle that strongly resembled a can of Michelob Dry. Richard Balducci, the publisher, explained that the spoof ad was a comment on environmental pollution. In particular, it referred to a recent spill of oil into the Gasconade River, from which Anheuser-Busch, the brewers of Michelob, drew its water supply.

Anheuser-Busch was not inclined to snicker. The company sued Balducci Publications for federal and state trademark infringement. A St Louis court rejected the claim, arguing that the 'advert' 'did not create a likelihood of confusion in the marketplace', but this decision was later reversed. A survey of 301 beer drinkers in various Missouri shopping malls had revealed that 45% were indeed confused, being unable to detect that the piece was a parody.

QUOTE UNQUOTE

Originality is nothing but judicious imitation. The most original writers borrowed one from another. The instruction we find in books is like fire. We fetch it from our neighbours, kindle it at home, communicate it to others, and it becomes the property of all.
Voltaire, French playwright

NAPSTER-PROOF BUT UNLISTENABLE

Heavy metal band Metallica released their eagerly awaited *Download This* CD in July 2000. The 74-minute CD consisted of one 55-minute song, entitled *Napster Begone*, and a 19-minute interview with drummer Lars Ulrich during which he answered one question. 'We realised that we couldn't stop the Napster movement, so we decided to make a Napster-proof album' he explained 'The *Napster Begone* track is so long and so horrible that no one in their right mind would take the time to download it. Our loyal fans will buy it though, because most have spent so much money on our merchandise that they can't afford a computer.'

*Initial trials of the Conversational Kipper
met with a mixed reception.*

AN ECONOMIST SPEAKS

Virtually unimaginable a half-century ago was the extent to which concepts and ideas would substitute for physical resources and human brawn in the production of goods and services. In 1948 radios were still being powered by vacuum tubes. Today, transistors deliver far higher quality with a mere fraction of the bulk. Fiber-optics has replaced huge tonnages of copper wire, and advances in architectural and engineering design have made possible the construction of buildings with much greater floor space but significantly less physical material than the buildings erected just after World War Two. Accordingly, while the weight of current economic output is probably only modestly higher than it was a half-century ago, value added, adjusted for price change, has risen well over threefold.

Alan Greenspan in a speech delivered in New York in October 1996

MONOPOLY MONEY

Monopoly, the board game invented by Charles B Darrow in 1933 gave the inventor a licence to print money. Parker Brothers purchased the rights a couple of years later, and the toy manufacturer now prints about $50 billion in Monopoly money every year, compared to the £70 billion or so real cash printed by the US Bureau of Printing and Engraving. Parker Brothers claims to have sold 200 million Monopoly sets during the game's 70-year history. On the basis that each US version contains $15,140, this implies a total print run of more than three trillion dollars.

GENERIC NAMES TO IDENTIFY

Which five of the following names have been deemed generic?

Land Rover	Polaroid
SPAM	Artex
Rollerblade	Formica
Aspirin	Etch-a-Sketch
Walkman	Nylon
Hoover	Aqua-Lung
Jeep	Transistor
Velcro	Brylcreem
Windsurfer	Jet Ski
Corn Flakes	Kerosene
Plasticine	Bubble Wrap

Answer on page 153.

PROFESSOR PAT PENDING

The Hannah-Barbera cartoon show *The Wacky Races*, first televised in 1968, featured 11 competitors. None had better credentials than Professor Pat Pending, creator of the awesome, metamorphosing Convert-a-Car. According to one compulsive archiver, Pending won three of the 34 races featured in the original series. He finished second twice and a creditable third on five occasions. Cumulatively, however, the Professor finished an embarrassing ninth of 11. The overall winners were the Neanderthal slag brothers in the Boulder Mobile. So much for technology.

For the record, the Anthill Mob came second in the Bullet-proof Bomb, followed by Rufus and Chainsaw in the Buzzwagon. The delicious Penelope Pitstop was seventh in the Compact Pussycat and the Army Surplus Special finished tenth. Dick Dastardly and his cackling hound Muttley brought up the rear.

BASMATI BATTLES

Basmati rice has been grown in the foothills of the Himalayas for hundreds, if not thousands, of years. There was therefore consternation in the Indian subcontinent when, in 1997, the United States Patent and Trademark Office (USPTO) issued Texas-based company RiceTec with 'varietal patents' for three strains of the fragrant, long-grained rice.

The Indian government responded by successfully challenging three of RiceTec's 20 novelty claims, and the company removed another 12 voluntarily. But the remaining five claims were enough to persuade the USPTO to confirm the patents in August 2001. It insisted, however, that RiceTec remove the word 'Basmati' from the titles of its products. Nevertheless, the company remained free to use the word in a generic sense in phrases such as 'Equal or superior to basmati'.

This was only a partial victory for India at best. As one former Minister of Agriculture observed, 'No variety of basmati rice can be developed without the original germplasm. At the very least.' Mr Sompal continued, 'India should get a royalty share of any such variety.'

QUOTE UNQUOTE

Scientia Donum Dei Est Unde Vendi Non Potest
('Knowledge is a gift from God, therefore it cannot be sold').
Medieval Canon Law Doctrine

US PATENT STATISTICS 1963–2003

To show the trend, we have selected each fourth year

Year	Applications	Grants	% grants with foreign origins
1963	90,982	48,971	18
1967	90,544	69,098	21
1971	111,095	81,790	28
1975	107,456	76,810	35
1979	108,209	52,412	38
1983	112,040	61,982	41
1987	139,455	89,385	47
1991	177,830	106,696	46
1995	228,238	113,834	43
1999	288,811	169,086	44
2003	342,441	187,017	47

Source: United States Patent and Trademark Office

30 *Year in the twentieth century in which Clarence Birdseye patented his technique for freezing*

The thing the Time Traveller held in his hand was a glittering metallic framework, scarcely larger than a small clock, and very delicately made. There was ivory in it, and some transparent crystalline substance… He took one of the small octagonal tables that were scattered about the room, and set it in front of the fire, with two legs on the hearthrug. On this table he placed the mechanism. Then he drew up a chair, and sat down…

'This little affair,' said the Time Traveller, resting his elbows upon the table and pressing his hands together above the apparatus, 'is only a model. It is my plan for a machine to travel through time. You will notice that it looks singularly askew, and that there is an odd twinkling appearance about this bar, as though it was in some way unreal.' He pointed to the part with his finger. 'Also, here is one little white lever, and here is another.'

'…Now I want you clearly to understand that this lever, being pressed over, sends the machine gliding into the future, and this other reverses the motion. This saddle represents the seat of a time traveller. Presently I am going to press the lever, and off the machine will go. It will vanish, pass into future Time, and disappear. Have a good look at the thing. Look at the table too, and satisfy yourselves there is no trickery. I don't want to waste this model, and then be told I'm a quack.'

… The Time Traveller put forth his finger towards the lever. 'No,' he said suddenly. 'Lend me your hand.' And turning to the Psychologist, he took that individual's hand in his own and told him to put out his forefinger. So that it was the Psychologist himself who sent forth the model Time Machine on its interminable voyage. We all saw the lever turn. I am absolutely certain there was no trickery. There was a breath of wind, and the lamp flame jumped. One of the candles on the mantel was blown out, and the little machine suddenly swung round, became indistinct, was seen as a ghost for a second perhaps, as an eddy of faintly glittering brass and ivory; and it was gone—vanished! Save for the lamp the table was bare.

HG Wells, *The Time Machine*

IT'S A BEAUTIFUL DAY

The song *Beautiful Day* from U2's album *All That You Can't Leave Behind* lends itself naturally to commercial licensing, with its dynamic, positive energy. But the specific ways in which it is used in different countries is revealing about national characteristics. In the UK, *Beautiful Day* is used to introduce the football on ITV; in the USA, it introduced John Kerry.

Erno Rubik

Cube mania was one of the defining features of the early 1980s. It is estimated that an eighth of the world's population has played with Erno Rubik's infuriating but compelling toy.

Rubik was born in Budapest in 1944. His parents were ideal for a budding inventor: his mother was a poet and a 'dreamer' and his father an engineer-mechanic. Erno studied sculpture for his first degree, but then switched to architecture at the Academy of Applied Arts and Design. He was teaching interior design there when he came up with the invention that would change his life.

In the spring of 1974, Rubik was wrestling with the structural problem of designing a block of cubes in which each cube was able to move independently without the whole falling apart. At first he experimented with rubber bands, but the solution was to have the blocks hold themselves together by virtue of their shapes. Soon he had constructed a cube made up of 26 'cubes' (not 27 as it appeared from the outside, as the one the middle was 'missing'). He marked each side with a different colour and started twisting. It took him a month to get back the original pattern.

Rubik applied for a Hungarian patent in January 1975, receiving approval two years later. The first cubes appeared in the shops towards the end of 1977. Sales were slow until an entrepreneur named Tibor Laczi saw a waiter fiddling with one while having having a coffee. He immediately traced the device to Rubik and arranged a meeting. 'I felt like giving him some money', he later recalled. 'He looked like a beggar. He was terribly dressed, and he had a cheap Hungarian cigarette hanging out of his mouth. But I knew I had a genius on my hands. I told him we could sell millions.'

The following day, Tibor went to the state trading company to seek permission to market the Cube in the West. Then he took it to the Nuremberg toy fair and wandered around playing with it. Here he bumped into British toy expert Tom Kremer, who was entranced, and subsequently ordered a million. Before long, Rubik had become the Eastern Block's first self-made millionaire.

Since 1977, over 100 million Cubes have been sold worldwide. Rubik has since invented other mind-bending puzzles, including the Snake, the Triamid, the Soma Cube and Magic Rings, but none has captured the world's imagination in the same way as the device that drove so many of us demented during the 1980s.

LANDMARKS IN THE HISTORY
OF GENETIC PATENTS

In 2003, scientists in the state of Iowa successfully cloned a banteng, an endangered cow-like species from the jungles of South East Asia. The clone was grown from a single cell taken from a captive animal in San Diego zoo which had died 23 years earlier. The surrogate mother was a regular cow.

'It let out a big bellow and everybody cheered', said scientist Robert Lanza of the banteng. The event was heralded for its potential value in the battle to save endangered species.

In the same year, the Human Genome Project was completed two years ahead of schedule. As of 2003, over 20,000 genes, 7,810 of them human, had been patented in the USA.

8 INVENTIONS WE COULD
POSSIBLY HAVE DONE WITHOUT

The Parking Meter • The Speed Camera
Sleeping Policemen • Polyphonic Ringtones
Call Waiting • Car Alarms
Automated Answering Services
Mondays

WELL DEFINED

Polo

Erroneously perceived by many as a sport involving ponies, chukkas and Prince Charles, this is in fact a proprietary brand of sports/leisure wear, according to lawyers representing Ralph Lauren, who in 2000 forced the US Polo association to change the name of their official magazine.

US PATENTS BY NUMBERS

1	Traction wheels (1836)
12	Improvements in trusses for cure of prolapsus uteri (1839)
123	Improvement in machine for weighing bodies (1837)
1,234	Mode of supplying water to locomotives (1839)
12,345	Lifting jack for moving rail cars (1865)
123,456	Improvement in blackboards (1872)
1,234,567	Soft collar (1917)

Bizarrely, the plagiarist at the wrong end of Ireland's first recorded intellectual property ruling was also one of the country's greatest saints. Columba (Columcille in Gaelic), a grandson of the great king Niall, was born in Donegal in 521. He received his religious training from St Finnian of Moville at the head of Strangford Loch. While he was at the monastery, Columba made a secret copy of Finnian's psalter. When the abbot-saint found out, he insisted that his pupil hand it over. Columba refused, arguing that he had done no harm to the original and that Finnian should not hinder the reproduction of the Scriptures for the dissemination of the faith.

The dispute was referred to the High King Diarmuid, who ruled that the copied psalter should be handed over to Finnian immediately. Clearly a rustic man, Diarmuid framed his declaration in earthy terms: 'To every cow her calf and to every book her copy!' he announced. Thus was the principle of copyright established in the Emerald Isle.

Columba was outraged, and persuaded the Niall clan to rise up against Diarmuid. Matters came to a head at Cooldrevny in 561, where three thousand men were killed. Diarmuid, utterly defeated, was forced to flee, and Columba got his psalter back.

Postscript: The Irish Synod decided that Columba was personally responsible for the deaths at Cooldrevny, and voted to exile him. So in 563, he clambered into a wickerwork boat with 12 disciples and sailed to the island of Iona off the west coast of Scotland. From this base, he orchestrated the conversion of the Picts and Scots.

CELEBRITY INVENTORS

Steve McQueen

Steve McQueen (born Indiana, 24 March 1930) came from a broken home, became a juvenile delinquent when his family moved to Los Angeles, and was only saved from a life of crime by a spell in a reform school after he was caught stealing hubcaps. After his discharge, McQueen drifted to Hollywood, where he went on to star in some great movies (*Papillon, The Thomas Crown Affair, The Magnificent Seven*).

Like many film stars (including James Dean and Paul Newman), McQueen loved the thrill of fast driving, and became well known as a racing car driver. But he found the seats excruciatingly uncomfortable. So he designed one which followed the contours of the human back. On 8 December 1969, he filed for a patent for his invention: the bucket seat. The seats were an instant hit and are now standard fixtures in sports and Grand Prix vehicles.

7 SHAPE MARKS

The shapes of the following products are all registered as trademarks or service marks in the United States:

Mickey Mouse Ears hat
Hershey's Kiss candy
The Weber barbeque grill
ET doll
The Coca-Cola bottle
Dustbuster vacuum cleaner
Igloo portable container
The Oscar Mayer Wienermobile

BARBIE QUEUE

Barbie is an icon, so when San Francisco artist Paul Hansen started selling bespoke versions of the doll in the city's Castro district in the mid-1990s, they flew off the shelf. But the manufacturers, Mattel Inc, were less than amused at seeing their pride and joy transformed into, among other alteregos, Trailer Trash Barbie, Drag Queen Barbie, Big Dyke Barbie, Exorcist Barbie and Tonya Harding Barbie. The company filed suit for copyright infringement, claiming a mere US$1.2 billion in damages. Hansen had sold about 150 of the dolls, for an overall profit of US$2,000.

Although art is sometimes deemed immune from copyright litigation, Hansen decided to back down. He promised to restrict the sale of the dolls to art galleries and to donate the proceeds to charity. But this failed to satisfy Mattel's lawyers, who wanted a tighter definition of 'art gallery' and some damages from the defendant. After a year of litigation, the judge issued a partial summary judgement against the company, accusing Mattel of 'not having a sense of humour'. But the ruling still left Hansen in a tight spot. He eventually settled out of court, agreeing to abandon all commercial use of the dolls. 'It's been a year from hell', he admitted.

WHAT'S HE ON ABOUT?

Which familiar device is the inventor describing in this excerpt from a US patent application?
'My present invention consists in the employment of a vibratory or undulatory current of electricity in contradistinction to a merely intermittent or pulsatory current, and of a method of, and apparatus for, producing electrical undulations upon the line-wire.'
Answer on page 153.

If nature has made any one thing less susceptible than all others of exclusive property, it is the action of the thinking power called an idea, which an individual may exclusively possess as long as he keeps it to himself; but the moment it is divulged, it forces itself into the possession of everyone, and the receiver cannot dispossess himself of it. Its peculiar character, too, is that no one possesses the less, because every other possesses the whole of it. He who receives an idea from me, receives instruction himself without lessening mine; as he who lights his taper at mine, receives light without darkening me. That ideas should freely spread from one to another over the globe, for the moral and mutual instruction of man, and improvement of his condition, seems to have been peculiarly and benevolently designed by nature, when she made them, like fire, expansible over all space, without lessening their density at any point, and like the air in which we breathe, move, and have our physical being, incapable of confinement or exclusive appropriation. Inventions then cannot, in nature, be a subject of property.'

Thomas Jefferson in a letter to Isaac McPherson in 1813

QUOTE UNQUOTE

If this company were to be split up, I would be glad to take the brands, trademarks, and goodwill, and you could have all the bricks and mortar... and I would fare better than you.
John Stuart, Chairman of Quaker Oats Ltd

BUSH BLOWS

In 1999, Zack Exley, a graduate student at the University of Massachusetts-Amherst, spotted that the domain names gwbush.com, gwbush.org and gbush.org had yet to be registered. This gave him a unique opportunity to rile his least favourite candidate in the forthcoming presidential election. Using the unclaimed addresses, he set up a satirical website to poke fun at the Bush campaign. Dubbya's lawyers threatened to sue Exley if he continued to use copyrighted and trademarked Republican images on the site. Mr Exley obliged, although his site remained critical of the campaign. But the episode had seriously unnerved the Bush team, and to pre-empt similar shenanigans, it proceeded to purchase 260 domain names that might conceivably be used against it. The president is now the proud owner of bushsucks.com, bushbites.com, bushblows.com and many http addresses in a similar vein.

For more than a century, two companies have been fighting over the marketing rights to the brand name 'Budweiser'.

In the blue corner we have the world's biggest brewery, Anheuser-Busch, which has been making a beer called 'Budweiser' since 1876. Depending on who you listen to, the founder of the company, Adolph Busch, either picked the name at random while looking at a map of southern Bohemia, or named his lager in a fit of nostalgia for a glass he had consumed there 11 years earlier. Anyhow, he registered the name 'Budweiser' as a US trademark.

In the red corner we have the tiny Budejovicky Budvar company, hailing from the Czech city of Ceske Budejovice, or Budweis as it is known in German. The brewery was established in 1895, 19 years after Anheuser-Busch began producing 'Budweiser'. But the local beer had always been called 'Budweiser', and the company saw no reason to break with tradition.

Round 1: 1911 The rivals agree to divide the world into two spheres of influence. Budvar will refrain from selling its beer north of the Panama Canal, Anheuser-Busch will do likewise in Europe.

Round 2: 1976 The Czech company launches a bid to prevent Anheuser-Busch registering either 'Budweiser' or 'Bud' as a UK trademark. It takes 12 years, but they are eventually successful. Until the UK registrar does a U-turn and allows Anheuser-Busch to register the name 'Bud'.

Round 3: 1979 The US brewery attempts to prevent the Czechs from using either name in the UK, on the grounds of passing off. The courts dismiss this claim, arguing (correctly) that British drinkers are aware of both products and are discerning enough to know which one they wanted.

Round 4: The Swiss courts block Anheuser-Busch from using either name in Switzerland, on the grounds that 'Budweiser' indicates the place of origin in a similar way to 'champagne'.

Round 5: The Iron Curtain dissolves. During the 1990s, Budvar expands into new territories. The Americans start to get nervous.

Round 6: A frenzy of punches and counter punches. Budvar claims victories in South Korea, Japan, New Zealand, Latvia, Australia, and Denmark. Anheuser-Busch wins in Argentina, Australia, Brazil, Denmark, Finland, Nigeria, Hungary, Italy, New Zealand, South Africa, Spain, Sweden and Tajikistan. Some of those countries are in both lists. Everyone is confused.

Round 7: An ambiguous round. Budvar finally achieves a presence in the US market, after an absence of six decades, but at the price of changing its name. 'Czechvar' receives US Patent Office approval in 2002.

Round 8: At the time of writing, the rivals are battling it out in the courts of more than 40 countries. Neither shows any sign of flagging. The argument may rumble on for eternity.

PLAGIARISM

The term 'plagiarism' derives from the Latin *plagium*, meaning 'kidnapping', and was first used in English in its modern context by the playwright Ben Jonson. Prior to Jonson's coinage, a 'plagiary' was somebody who kidnapped a child or a slave.

THE POWER OF COPYRIGHT-FREE SONG TITLES

To underline the point that song titles are, by and large, uncopyrightable, here are four melodically unrelated songs all called 'The Power of Love'. Writing one seems to have been compulsory during the early 1980s:

Jennifer Rush	*The Power of Love* (1985)
(Celine Dion covered this version in 1993)	
Huey Lewis and the News	*The Power of Love* (1985)
Frankie Goes to Hollywood	*The Power of Love* (1984)
Luther Vandross	*The Power of Love* (1981)

WELL DEFINED

Pi

Mathematical truths are usually considered beyond the scope of intellectual property law, but this notion was challenged at the end of the nineteenth century in the Midwest. Although the ratio of a circle's circumference to its diameter is widely agreed to be somewhere in the region of 3.14159, this was not the view of a certain Edward Goodwin of Solitude, Indiana (an appropriate address given his approach to mathematics). In 1897, Dr Goodwin submitted a bill for the consideration of the State Assembly that proposed an entirely different value for Pi. Unfortunately (or perhaps deliberately), he expressed his argument in such obscure mathematical terms that no one can be quite sure what he was getting at. Many experts have argued that 'Goodwin's Pi' was 3.2. The *Guinness Book of World Records* goes for a round four. Either way, the law would have made life difficult for the state's builders and engineers.

The motive behind this surprising piece of would-be legislation was, of course, financial. Under Goodwin's proposal, residents of Indiana would have 'enjoyed' free use of his discovery, while everyone else would have had to pay a royalty. But it wasn't to be. A university professor named Clarence Waldo happened to be in the building while the bill was being debated. Horrified by what he was hearing, he convened the senators and gave them a crash-course in geometry. Goodwin's bill was thrown out.

TOE PUPPET

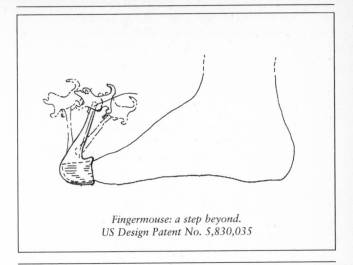

Fingermouse: a step beyond.
US Design Patent No. 5,830,035

5 COLOUR MARKS REGISTERED IN THE US

1. The copper band at the top of a Duracell battery
2. The translucent tips of Shakespeare fishing rods
3. McDonald's striped, red, white and gold french fry container
4. The green body, yellow wheel combination of John Deere tractors
5. Burberry plaid

THE FROWNY EMOTICON

On 2 January 2001, Despair, Inc announced that the United States Patent and Trademark Office (USPTO) had awarded them a registered trademark for their logo, the 'frowny' emoticon. Despair's Chief Operating Officer, Dr EL Kersten, told reporters at a press conference that the company intended to sue 'anyone and everyone who uses the so-called 'frowny' emoticon, or our trademarked logo, in their written email correspondence. Ever.'

Andrew Kirkus, co-editor of *IP Magazine*, assessed the episode thus: 'Whether the issuance is a dangerous one remains to be seen. What is certain, however, is that it appears that someone has finally bested patent 5443036 for the most ridiculous intellectual property filing in history.'

US Patent No. 5443036, incidentally, is for a method of exercising cats using a beam of light invisible to humans but fascinating to felines.

ELAINE'S INVENTIONS

Elaine Vassal (played by Jane Krakowski) is the office secretary at Fish Cage Associates, the fictitious law firm for which Ally McBeal (Calista Flockhart) works in the eponymous Fox television series. Elaine is a complex character: on the surface she's a tarty, attention-seeking busybody, but underneath she's sensitive, lonely and wise. Above all (and here we come to the point), she's a very creative inventor. Here are a few Elaine specials:

1. **The Face Bra** – a brassiere-like garment, worn over the head, to support the face when jogging. The idea was to prevent wrinkle-creating movement of the cheeks, nose and lips. Although it made the wearer look, in Ally McBeal's words, 'like Hannibal Lecter', the Face Bra evidently struck a chord among vainer joggers. Elaine made quite a lot of money from the device, obtaining a patent and starring in her own infomercial. (Later a relative came out of the woodwork and claimed that Elaine had stolen the idea from her daughter. But that's another story…)

2. **Ice Goggles** – Specs packed with ice, for tired or morning-after eyes.

3. **Automatic Toilet Seat Warmer** – fairly self-explanatory.

4. **The Husband CD** – an audio substitute for a man about the house.

QUOTE UNQUOTE

A Book is the Author's Property, 'tis the Child of his Inventions, the Brat of the Brain.
Daniel Defoe, author

SILLY PUTTY

The invention of Silly Putty was a side effect of the US's attempts to cope with the rubber shortage brought about the Japanese capture of producer-nations during World War Two. In 1943, James Wright, a Scottish engineer, was working at General Electric's laboratory in New Haven, Connecticut, to find a viable method of producing synthetic rubber. One day he mixed some silicon oil and boric acid in a test tube. When he removed the gooey substance that formed inside, Wright threw a lump to the floor and found that it bounced back up again. After circulating among chemists for a few years, Silly Putty was launched as a children's novelty item in 1949. Since then, over 200 million plastic eggs-full of the stuff have been sold worldwide.

Until the late nineteenth century, when the concept of copyright began to be extended to 'the substance and not the form alone', American law defined 'copying' very narrowly. In 1853, a federal circuit judge rejected Harriet Beecher Stowe's allegation that a German translation of *Uncle Tom's Cabin* had infringed her copyright. 'By the publication of Mrs Stowe's book,' he ruled, 'the creations of the genius and imagination of the author have become as much public property as those of Homer or Cervantes... All her conceptions and inventions may be used and abused by imitators, playwrights and poetasters... A translation may, in loose phraseology, be called a transcript or copy of her thoughts, but in no correct sense can it be called a copy of her book.'

LANDMARKS IN THE HISTORY
OF GENETIC PATENTS

In February 2000, a baby rabbit named Alba was born in Jouy-en-Josas in France. Alba had been engineered with a fluorescence-producing jellyfish gene, and had been created as the centrepiece of the GFP ('green fluorescent protein') Bunny art project, organised by Eduardo Kac of the Art Institute of Chicago. Although Kac wanted to stimulate debate, he was keen to emphasise that Alba's 'social' integration was a crucial part of the project. 'Transgenic art' he declared, '...is a new art form based on the use of genetic engineering to transfer natural or synthetic genes to an organism, to create unique living beings. This must be done with great care, with acknowledgment of the complex issues thus raised and, above all, with a commitment to respect, nurture, and love the life thus created.'

It should be emphasised that Alba, who became a much-loved family pet, only glowed under blue light of a specific wavelength.

THOUGHTS ON LAVATORIES

In the year 2000, St Lawrence's church near Doncaster in Yorkshire paid an unlikely tribute to a local inventor. Thomas Crapper, a Victorian sanitary engineer famous for improving the design of the flush toilet, was commemorated via a small silhouette of his celebrated invention embedded in a new stained-glass window. 'Officials thought a white loo might stand out too much in the window and become the focus of attention instead of Christ in Majesty,' explained a project coordinator.

In case you're wondering, Crapper did not lend his name to an unmentionable item associated with his life's work. The term had been around for centuries already, but he was the subject of a biography entitled *Flushed with Success*.

ERIC CORLEY, MASTER HACKER

Eric Corley, aka Emmanuel Goldstein (after the leader of the underground movement in Orwell's *1984*), has been a major thorn in the side of the intellectual property protection industry for decades. Corley is the publisher of *2600: The Hacker Quarterly*, the bible of the hacking community. The '2600' refers to a discovery made by proto-hackers during the 1960s: by transmitting tones of 2600 hertz across certain long distance phone lines, they found they could access 'operator mode'. The number also features in the names of Corley's company (2600 Enterprises, Inc) and website (2600.com, online since 1995). Corley has described it as a 'mystical thing'.

A glance at some of the articles that have appeared in the magazine or on the website should explain why Mr Corley makes corporate America nervous. Past topics have included advice on accessing other people's emails, installing Linux on your Xbox, stealing domain names, intercepting mobile phone calls and breaking into the computer systems of Federal Express and Costco.

In January 2000, the communications industry bit back. Eight Hollywood studios, all members of Motion Picture Association of America (MPAA), successfully sued Corley and two associates for posting a DVD decryption code on 2600.com. The arrival in court of a posse of teenage hackers wearing T-shirts adorned with the forbidden code failed to sway Judge Lewis A Kaplan.

Despite this setback, Corley and his magazine and website continue to thrive.

SMART USES OF COUNTRY-CODES

ba.be • click.it • co.at
ge.org • glo.be • inter.net
ja.net • like.it • look.at
read.it • sci.fi • see.it
stop.it • this.is

LIBYA DISAPPEARS FROM THE INTERNET

On April 13 2004, Libya suddenly disappeared from the internet. For four days, all .ly domain names were mysteriously inaccessible, to the considerable chagrin of the 12,500-odd organisations that had paid $500 a pop for internet addresses registered in Libya. It later transpired that the source of the problem had been a dispute within the country about who owned the rights to sell the suffix.

US patent number for a chandelier formed by three fish-shaped lamps or reservoirs (1836)

'Just protecting against cyber squatters while we're away...'

NATIONS FILING THE MOST PATENT APPLICATIONS UNDER THE PATENT COOPERATION TREATY

Top 10 countries of origin (2002 filings)		Number of applications	Percentage share of total
US	United States of America	44,609	39.1
DE	Germany	15,269	13.4
JP	Japan	13,531	11.9
GB	United Kingdom	6,274	5.5
FR	France	4,877	4.3
NL	Netherlands	4,019	3.5
SE	Sweden	2,988	2.6
KR	Republic of Korea	2,552	2.2
CH&LI	Switzerland & Liechtenstein	2,469	2.2
CA	Canada	2,210	1.9

Source: WIPO

Number of UK patents awarded to the UK Secretary for Defence in 2003 43

HP Sauce

HP Sauce was invented by a Nottingham grocer named FG Garton. He began marketing the spicy, fruity sauce in 1903. Garton gave it the name 'HP' after learning that it was served in one of the restaurants in the Houses of Parliament in London. He later sold the brand and recipe to Edwin Samson Moore, owner of the Midland Vinegar Company, for £150.

The sauce received another political boost in the 1960s, when Mary Wilson, the wife of the then prime minister, revealed to the *Sunday Times* that 'If Harold has a fault, it is that he will drown everything with HP Sauce'. The result was a new nickname: 'Wilson's Gravy'.

HP sauce is now owned by Danone.

LEGAL TEASERS

**Link the following novels with the books
that allegedly 'inspired' them:**

(a) *The Rachel Papers* by Martin Amis
(b) *The Wind Done Gone* by Alice Randall
(c) *The Life of Pi* by Yahn Martell
(d) *Rebecca* by Daphne du Maurier
(e) The *Harry Potter* novels by JK Rowling
(f) *Last Orders* by Graham Swift

(a) *As I Lay Dying* by William Faulkner
(b) *The Legend of Rah and the Muggles* by Nancy Stouffer
(c) *Gone with the Wind* by Margaret Mitchell
(d) *Wild Oats* by Jason Epstein
(e) *Max and the Cats* by Moacyr Scliar
(f) *The Successor* by Carolina Nabuco

Answer on page 153.

AAAAAARGH!

Valentine's Day 1876 was not a happy one for Elisha Gray. On that day, he filed a 'caveat' (an announcement of an intention to patent an invention within three months) for a device that would later be known as the telephone. Incredibly, Gray later learned that Alexander Graham Bell had submitted a patent application for a similar device only hours beforehand. Bell was eventually awarded the relevant patent after a protracted legal dispute. With hindsight, perhaps Gray should have booked an alarm call.

BEN JONSON'S EPIGRAM
TO PROULE THE PLAGIARY

> Forbear to tempt me Proule, I will not show
>   A Line unto thee, till the World it know;
> Or that I have by two good sufficient Men,
>   To be the wealthy Witness of my Pen:
> For all thou hear'st, thou swear'st thy self didst do.
>   Thy Wit lives by it, Proule, and Belly too.
> Which, if thou leave not soon (though I am loth)
>   I must a Libel make, and cozen* both.

* To 'cozen' is to cheat or dupe. Jonson means to cheat both Proule's wit (by denying him sight of his verses) and his belly (by refusing to give him dinner).

SMART SAMPLING

Modern record companies find themselves spending a great deal of time and money clearing samples. But there is an elegant solution: they can simply buy the rights. And because the most sampled songs are obscure soul and funk numbers from the 1960s and 1970s, this can be surprisingly cheap.

A good example of the practice is provided by Tuff City Records of New York, which purchased the rights to The Honey Drippers' 1973 track *Impeach the President* largely because so many of its artists had sampled the song. This turned out to be good business: the record has been sampled by more than 100 performers, and Tuff City finds itself in a no-lose position. If the sampler is signed up with the company, it has no royalties to pay. If an artist from another label wishes to sample *Impeach the President*, they have to pay Tuff City.

SPOT THE DIFFERENCE –
THE MULLET THAT FLOUNDERED

Can you spot the differences between these two songs:

> *Love is a Wonderful Thing* (Michael Bolton, 1991)
> *Love is a Wonderful Thing* (The Isley Brothers, 1966)

In 1994, the Supreme Court found Bolton guilty of having plagiarised the earlier song despite his protestations that he had never heard it. Notwithstanding the coincidence of the titles, the basis for the claim lay in musical rather than lyrical similarities between the songs. Bolton was ordered to pay a massive US$5.4 million to the defendants, the biggest damages award ever made in a music-related plagiarism case.

What is a former Patent Office employee to do with all the free time suddenly on his hands when he retires? The late, great Arthur Pedrick of Sussex decided to put his extensive knowledge of patent application procedure to good practical use: he crossed over to the other side. Between 1962 and 1977, Pedrick patented 162 inventions, each one wackier than the last. He was undaunted by the fact that none of them were taken up commercially. It seemed almost beside the point.

The breadth of Mr Pedrick's vision is well demonstrated by his radiation detector (UK Patent No. 1426698, 1976). Depending on how the device was set up, it could either a) detect a nuclear explosion from an orbiting satellite and automatically dump a 1000 megaton atom bomb on the aggressor nation, or b) allow Arthur's cat Ginger to pass through a cat flap while freezing out unwanted feline visitors. The machine worked by detecting the character of the light falling on it from a given source. When it registered the pre-selected wavelength, a release mechanism was triggered. History fails to reveal whether Ginger ever got his high-tec flap, but we do know that discussions he held with his master on the subject of nuclear physics made their way into the official patent documentation.

Other classic Pedrick inventions include an amphibious bicycle, a steerable golf ball and an apparatus allowing a car to be driven from the back seat. But his most ambitious project was a scheme to irrigate the world's deserts. With admirable simplicity, he reasoned that some parts of the planet were much too dry while others had huge and redundant supplies of water. The solution was to fire a constant stream of snowballs from the polar icecaps into needy desert regions via a network of giant peashooters.

Eventually, running the 'One-Man-Think-Tank Basic Research Laboratories of Sussex' began to take its toll. Mrs Pedrick grew weary of the cost of her husband's patent applications, not to mention the houseful of mechanical junk, and prevailed on him to curtail his inventive activities.

QUOTE UNQUOTE

He who builds a better mousetrap these days runs into material shortages, patent-infringement suits, work stoppages, collusive bidding, discount discrimination – and taxes.
HE Martz, engineering specialist

OH-OH SAY CAN YOU CIG

*A Stars and Stripes cigarette, just the thing for a
nicotine-starved American expat on the 4th of July.
UK Design Patent No. 2071091.*

INTELLECTUAL PROPERTY PARADOXES

Patent law seeks to promote economic activity by granting exclusion
rights to inventors. Anti-trust law seeks to promote economic activity
by denying the very same rights.

THE MAE WEST BOTTLE

In 1915, the Root Glass Company of Terre Haut, Indiana, answered
the Coca-Cola company's call for a 'bottle which a person will
recognise as a Coca-Cola bottle even if he feels it in the dark. The
Coca-Cola bottle should be shaped that, even if broken, one could tell
at a glance what it was.' The design was inspired by an illustration
of a kola nut in a recent edition of the *Encyclopedia Britannica*.

The new bottle was quickly christened the 'Mae West' in homage to the equally curvaceous film star. It has been intimately tied
up with American popular culture ever since. During World War
Two, one of General Eisenhower's first actions on landing in Africa
was to send a telegram requesting 'eight Coca-Cola bottling plants
immediately'. In 1962, the designer Raymond Loewy built a fibre-
glass car, the Studebaker Avanti, whose contours were openly modelled on those of the Mae West. During the 1960s, Andy Warhol
described the bottle as 'the design icon of the decade', even though
it was half a century old. The Coca-Cola bottle was also the UK's
first registered three-dimensional trademark.

Thus far in its history, the Coca-Cola Company has manufactured
about 850 billion of the bottles.

SPITTING IMAGE

During the 1980s and early 1990s, several British celebrities were tormented by the unflattering latex versions of themselves which appeared on the satirical television show *Spitting Image*. Roy Hattersley, the former Deputy Leader of the Labour party, was particularly disturbed by his puppet, which spewed spittle like a geyser. But only one 'victim' was ever moved to take legal action against the programme. In 1985, Norris McWhirter, the co-founder of the *Guinness Book of World Records*, brought an unsuccessful action against the Independent Broadcasting Authority (the show's broadcaster) for depicting his head atop a nude female torso. The prevailing legal opinion was that the item was legitimate satire. As Mr McWhirter was born an identical twin, his discomfort at seeing his own face on someone else's shoulders came as something of a surprise.

OASIS

The following enterprises are all named Oasis, although they operate in different commercial/geographical spheres:

- A rock band featuring the heavy-eyebrowed Gallagher brothers.
- A swimming pool complex in Swindon, Wiltshire.
- A UK soft drinks manufacturer
- A UK fashion retailer
- A water-cooler manufacturer from Colombus, Ohio
- A trademarked 'wound matrix' dressing manufactured by Healthpoint Ltd of Fort Worth, Texas
- A San Francisco based company manufacturing small animal and bird sanitary water dispensers

ECONOMIC ESPIONAGE

The US National Counterintelligence Agency estimates that US business loses around US$50 billion a year through economic espionage. In recent years, big companies whose employees have been prosecuted for stealing trade secrets have included Gillette, Deloitte & Touche, Bristol-Myers, Harvard Medical School and Boeing. In the fast-moving high-tech sector, getting hold of somebody else's innovation can bring substantial reward before anyone notices that it's gone. Lawsuits alleging theft of trade secrets have recently been brought by Apple, by British mobile phone maker Sendo against Microsoft, and by dozens of pay TV broadcasters in Europe and the US against NDS, News Corporation's British-based maker of the smart cards that decode encrypted pay TV signals.

PRIORITIES FOR TIME-TRAVELLERS

Hank, the narrator, has travelled back 13 centuries in time after receiving a blow to the head. By correctly predicting the date of an eclipse, he escapes a death sentence and secures an important position at court.

They were always having grand tournaments there at Camelot; and very stirring and picturesque and ridiculous human bull-fights they were, too, but just a little wearisome to the practical mind. However, I was generally on hand – for two reasons: a man must not hold himself aloof from the things which his friends and his community have at heart if he would be liked – especially as a statesman; and both as business man and statesman I wanted to study the tournament and see if I couldn't invent an improvement on it. That reminds me to remark, in passing, that the very first official thing I did, in my administration – and it was on the very first day of it, too – was to start a patent office; for I knew that a country without a patent office and good patent laws was just a crab, and couldn't travel any way but sideways or backways.

…The first thing you want in a new country, is a patent office; then work up your school system; and after that, out with your (news)paper.

Mark Twain, *A Connecticut Yankee in King Arthur's Court,*
one of the first books to use the idea of time travel

QUOTE UNQUOTE

Art is either plagiarism or revolution.
Paul Gauguin, French painter

INTELLECTUAL PROPERTY SYMBOLS

©	Copyright
®	Registered Trademark
™	Trademark (in US denotes registration applied for)
SM	Service Mark
Æ	Phonograph or other copyrighted sound recording
'U' in a circle	Certified as kosher by the Union of Orthodox Jewish Congregations of America
'M' in a circle	Mask Work

A Mask Work is a work protected by the US Semiconductor Chip Protection Act. The Act was designed to prevent firms stripping rivals' chips, photographing each layer and using the photos as the basis for constructing copies. In any event, hardly anyone bothered to register their products as mask works, or indeed to try to pirate chips in the first place. Technology moved on...

5 INVENTORS WHO CHOSE NOT TO PATENT

Wilhelm Roentgen – refused to commercially exploit his discovery of x-rays.

Jonas Salk – when asked who owned the patent for the polio vaccine he had developed in 1952, he replied: 'The people. Could you patent the sun?'

John Walker – declined to patent the matches he invented in 1827, or 'sulphuretted peroxide strikables' as the yard-long sticks were described.

Pierre and Marie Curie – refused to patent their process for refining radium. Marie declared that radium 'is a natural chemical, it is for the people'.

Volvo – the Swedish car manufacturer made its 'lap and diagonal' seatbelt freely available to competitors.

QUOTE UNQUOTE

Nothing can be made of nothing; he who has laid up no materials can produce no combinations.
Sir Joshua Reynolds, English portrait painter

THE 'REAL' PROFESSOR CALCULUS

Anyone who has read Hergé's Tintin books will be familiar with the lovable, stone-deaf inventor Professor Cuthbert Calculus. But few will be aware that he was modelled on a real character. Auguste Piccard was a Swiss physics professor from the University of Brussels who didn't just conform to the stereotype of the absent-minded scientist. With his goatee beard, pebble glasses, unkempt hair and otherworldly ways, he went a long way towards creating it.

Piccard's greatest claim to fame was as the inventor of the sealed, pressurised capsule. This allowed him to make the first manned assault on the stratosphere. On 27 May 1931, he ascended to 51,000 feet in an enormous hydrogen balloon called the 'FNRS', wearing an inverted chicken basket as a helmet. During the ascent, the gondola whistled alarmingly as air rushed out through a tiny hole. Piccard calmly located it, plugged it with petroleum jelly and dribbled some liquid oxygen on the floor to replenish the cabin atmosphere.

When he had satisfied his curiosity about the skies, Piccard turned his attention to the deep and invented the bathyscaphe. This was, in effect, an underwater balloon, filled with lighter-than-water aviation fluid and using lead shot for ballast.

50 *Term in years of copyright protection for sound recordings and broadcasts in the EC*

ATHLETIC PATENTS?

In 1996, a group of intellectual property lawyers wrote an article for the US *National Law Journal*, arguing that athletic manoeuvres were appropriate subjects for patents. A method for skiing 10% faster, for example, was clearly a 'useful process' in certain contexts, such as trying to win a race. Similarly, athletic techniques could undoubtedly be non-obvious and novel.

Technically speaking, Robert M Kunstadt, F Scott Kieff, and Robert G Kramer certainly had a point, but their proposal seems unlikely to be taken up by the sporting world in the foreseeable future. The patenting of manoeuvres would play havoc with competition. As the Brits say, it just wouldn't be cricket.

THERE'S NO PLACE LIKE ROME

Around the turn of the millennium, a number of British companies decided to brand or re-brand themselves with faux Latin names. They were searching, no doubt, for a whiff of the grandeur and permanence of Ancient Rome:

OLD NAME	NEW NAME
Royal Mail	Consignia*
British Steel	Corus
British Gas	Centrica
Guinness**	Diageo
Norwich Union	Aviva

*the decision was quickly reversed
** we're simplifying matters here

AHEAD OF HIS TIME

Now, if there exists any incorporeal right or property in the author, detached from his manuscript, no act of publication can destroy it. Can then such right or property exist at all?... Abridgments of books, translations, notes, as effectually deprive the original author of the fruit of his labours, as direct particular copies, yet they are allowable. The composers of music, the engravers of copper-plates, the inventors of machines, are all excluded from the privilege now contended for; but why, if an equitable and moral right is to be the sole foundation of it? Their genius, their study, their labour, their originality, is as great as an author's, their inventions are as much prejudiced by copyists, and their claim, in my opinion, stands exactly on the same footing...

Lord Chief Justice De Grey, speaking in the House of Lords during the seminal Donaldson v. Beckett case, 1774. Composers, engravers and inventors are, of course, now catered for by IP law.

In September 1996, Ronald McDonald, a 61-year-old retired history teacher from Westhill in Aberdeen, threatened burger giant McDonald's with legal action for pinching his name. 'Frankly, I always feel a bit annoyed that my name is the same as a clown, especially when I read of this action by the company,' he announced. 'As far as I'm concerned they have stolen my name and my father's name for commercial purposes. To me it's an attack on the Scottish clan system. They have no right to claim the prefix Mc or Mac as theirs.' Mr McDonald wrote to the company's managing director to tell him: 'The prefix Mc and the name McDonald has been used in Scotland and spread worldwide many centuries before your firm was ever in existence.' He also enclosed a Doric poem.

The catalyst for McDonald's intervention was the burger company's threat to sue a small Buckinghamshire corner shop called McMunchies. But a spokesman claimed that he had misunderstood what they were doing. 'It's got nothing to do with the Mc prefix, other than in a food service context. We believe Ms Blair, the owner, is certainly seeking to confuse customers into thinking that there may be some association with McDonald's, particularly with our unique stylised writing, and we hope she will remove the Mc prefix from her shop. Of course the Mc isn't copyright when it's a family name, or a shoe shop or whatever'. Faced with the financial might of the restaurant chain, Mary Blair appears to have backed down.

Interestingly, Mr McDonald is known to his friends as 'Big Mac'.

PLANT PATENTS GRANTED IN US 1963–2003

To show the trend, we have selected each fourth year.

Year	Grants
1963	129
1967	85
1971	71
1975	150
1979	131
1983	197
1987	229
1991	353
1995	387
1999	420
2003	994

Source: United States Patent and Trademark Office

The world's first patent was arguably granted in 1421 to Filippo Brunelleschi for an improved method of transporting goods up and down the river Arno in Florence (a notoriously tricky business). In contrast to modern patents, the document is singularly vague about the nature of the invention. This is because Brunelleschi, architect of the magnificent dome of the city's cathedral, was so revered by the authorities that he was able to strike a deal on his own terms: he would only reveal the details of his brainchild once he had been granted a three-year monopoly.

The machine seems to have been a flat-keeled boat with paddle wheels, designed to be towed by smaller boats. It was unveiled in 1428, long after Brunelleschi's initial patent had expired. Nicknamed 'Il Badalone' ('The Monster'), the vessel was launched from Pisa with a cargo of 50 tonnes of Carrara marble. After 25 miles, disaster struck. Il Badalone sank and the entire load was lost. Brunelleschi never fully recovered.

Below are the salient portions of the patent:

'The Magnificent and Powerful Lords, Lords Magistrate, and Standard Bearer of Justice:

Considering that the admirable Filippo Brunelleschi... has invented some machine or kind of ship, by means of which he thinks he can easily, at any time, bring in any merchandise and load on the river Arno... and that he refuses to make such machine available to the public... [but would] if he enjoyed some prerogative concerning this... and desiring that this matter... shall be brought to light to be of profit to both said Filippo and our whole country... they deliberated on 19 June 1421;

That no person alive, wherever born and of whatever status, dignity, quality, and grade, shall dare or presume, within three years... to commit any of the following acts on... any... river, stagnant water, swamp, or water running or existing in the territory of Florence: to have, hold, or use in any manner... a machine or ship or other instrument designed to... transport on water any... goods, except such ship or machine or instrument as they may have used until now for similar operations... and further that any such new or newly shaped machine, etc. shall be burned;

Provided however that the foregoing shall not be held to cover, and shall not apply to, any newly invented or newly shaped machine, etc. designed to ship, transport or travel on water, which may be made by Filippo Brunelleschi or with his will and consent.'

ACCIDENTAL INVENTIONS

Stainless steel

Harry Brearley was working to prevent corrosion in rifle barrels when he accidentally invented something that would revolutionise the world of cutlery. Not an obvious route, but Brearley was an observant chap and he knew when he had made something worth keeping.

Brearley had a background in steel. His father was a steel melter and young Harry had followed his father into the industry. Through years of private study and night school he became an expert in the analysis of steel and in 1908, at the age of 37, was given the opportunity to set up the Brown Firth Laboratories for research purposes. It was under this guise that Brearley was given the job of looking at the problem of rifle barrels.

The rifle problem was simple: when the gun was fired, the heat and gases generated would quickly erode away the inner barrel. Brearley was given the task of finding a steel that would not erode away, and he instantly set about combining varying amounts of chromium with steel to fix the problem.

Brealey made history on 13 August 1913 when his mix of 0.24% carbon and 12.8% chromium with steel created the first ever stainless steel. And although Brealey didn't immediately realise what he had created, the resistance of the metal to acids such as vinegar and lemon juice soon pointed him in the right direction.

At that time cutlery was made from silver or carbon steel, or plated with nickel. None of which were resistant to rust, so Brealey launched his 'rustless steel' (later renamed as the more catchy 'stainless steel') on the world with great gusto.

But it was not all smooth sailing. Brearley was initially unable to interest his employers in his new steel, but once they saw how well the product was selling, Brown Firth Laboratories soon changed their mind, claiming that they owned the patent because Brearley was working for them at the time of his invention. The dispute unresolved, Brealey resigned from the company in 1915, and became works manager at another works in Sheffield where he continued to produce stainless steel.

SPACEWAR

Generally considered to be the first video game, Spacewar was developed in 1962 by Steve Russell, a student at the Massachussets Institute of Technology. It was a simple game involving two players firing lasers at one another. Unfortunately, the only machines able to run the programme at the time were mainframes the size of a house.

VICIOUS CIRCLES

There was once a theory that the law of trademarks and trade names was an attempt to protect the consumer against 'passing off' of inferior goods under misleading labels. Increasingly the courts have departed from any such theory... [they] have taken refuge in a vicious circle to which no obviously extra-legal facts can gain admittance... It purports to base legal protection upon economic value, when, as a matter of fact, the economic value of a sales device depends on the extent to which it will be legally protected.

Felix Cohen, 'Transcendental Nonsense and the Functional Approach' in *The Columbia Law Review*, 1935

IRRESISTIBLE DOMAIN NAMES

In May 2004, a character calling himself 'Twysted' offered to sell the following domain names via the internet. Unless otherwise noted, they were priced at five bucks each.

twysted-realmz.com – has one year left.
demented-gothicum.biz – has 1.5 years left.
hells-vistion.com – has one year left – reduced price for $2
stifler-inc.net – has one year left.
accessprograms-c-drive.com – has 1.7 years left.

If hells-vistion.com was really spelled like that, two dollars seems a bit steep.

PRINCESS DI P

In November 2001, the world premier of *Lady Di – Diana: A Smile that Enchants the World* took place in a half-empty theatre in Saarbruecken in Germany. The musical featured a scene that depicted Camilla Parker Bowles laughing at Diana's naivety while seducing Prince Charles. There was also a song in which an array of ghostly figures warned the princess of the dangers of walking around in fields of land-mines.

If Andre Engelhardt had had his way, the musical would never have been staged. Engelhardt had legally objected to the show's title, arguing that he 'owned' the phrase 'Lady Di' via his registered trademark for perfume and lingerie. But his argument had been rejected by a Munich court.

Afterwards, the court had issued a rueful statement revealing its discomfort at having to uphold the law in this instance:

'The description "Lady Di" is an unmistakable reference to the late Princess of Wales, even if this was not her proper name... The rights to use the name should only be seen as belonging to her heirs.'

Kitchener, I'm gonna sue you for copyright infringement!

INTELLECTUALS' PROPERTIES

Karl Marx	41 Maitland Park Road, London NW3	1875–83
Sigmund Freud	19 Bergasse, 1090 Vienna	1891–1938
Albert Einstein	112 Mercer Street, Princeton, NJ	1933–55
Sir Isaac Newton	35 St Martin's Street, London WC2	1710–27
Johann W. Goethe	Via del Corso 18, Rome	1786–88

YOU COULD TRY THIS WHEN
BOOK SHOPPING IN RIYADH . . .

Under traditional Islamic law, a person who stole a book was not subject to the usual penalty for theft, namely the amputation of the offending hand. This was because the light-fingered bibliophile was assumed to have been not after the paper and ink, but the intangible ideas that they embodied. All knowledge was held to come from Allah, therefore no mortal had the right to lay claim to it. In recent times, however, the Muslim legal world has tended to take a more 'Western' stance on intellectual property.

BACKWARD BEATLES

Which Beatles track is based on the first movement of Beethoven's Moonlight sonata played backwards?
Answer on page 153.

Answer on page 153.

FOGERTY V ZAENTZ

In 1985, a long-running feud between Creedance Clearwater Revival's John Fogerty and Fantasy Records supremo Saul Zaentz boiled over with the release of Fogerty's album *Centrefield*. Fogerty, who resented having signed the band's rights over to Zaentz during the 1970s, got his revenge with a song entitled *Zanz Can't Dance*, about a con man with pig's ears. Zaentz countered with a defamation suit, and then brought an action against Fogerty for plagiarising Creedance Clearwater Revival's *Run Through the Jungle* on another track, *The Old Man Down the Road*. In other words, Fogerty was accused of copying himself.

QUOTE UNQUOTE

Strangely enough, the one universal myth of America – Show Business – flowered in a desert where a bunch of barely educated immigrants hoped to find the right conditions for shooting cheap movies and respite from the owners of the patents for film equipment whom they were ripping off.
Frederic Raphael, 'A Writer Stalks the Hollywood Myth',
NewYork Times

FOOTBALLERS AND INTELLECTUAL PROPERTY

Ex-Manchester United star Eric Cantona is not a man to trifle with, as supporters of Crystal Palace will testify (during a match between the sides in 1995, he jumped over a barrier and kung fu kicked one of them, having reached his tolerance threshold for verbal abuse). Some people will never learn, however, and in 1996 Cantona launched proceedings against the owners of 'Cantona French Wines Limited' and 'Cantona French Brandy Limited' for passing off. Advertisements for their similarly named products had appeared in the newspapers accompanied by a phrase inextricably associated with Mr Cantona, namely 'Ooh Aah!' (For the uninitiated, this was the central motif of a popular chant devoted to him). To add insult to injury, the wine bottle was labelled with the number 7, just like Cantona's United shirt. The case was settled in the plaintiff's favour before it got to trial.

ORIGIN OF THE NAME

The 'John'

British visitors to the United States are frequently mystified by the local habit of referring to the lavatory as 'the John', particularly those who happen to be called 'John'. (Americans called 'Lou' experience similar difficulties when making the reverse journey). If they think about the expression at all, beyond desperately trying to decode it, they assume it is a modern and rather prissy American euphemism. But in fact it has a thoroughly British pedigree. The name derives from Sir John Harrington, who invented a flushing toilet in 1596 for his godmother Queen Elizabeth I. He published instructions for building similar devices in a pamphlet entitled 'The Metamorphosis of Ajax', a 'jakes' being a contemporary word for the smallest room in the house.

QUOTE UNQUOTE

Genius is the introduction of a new element into the intellectual universe: or, if that be not allowed, it is the application of powers to objects on which they had not before been exercised, or the employment of them in such a manner as to produce effects hitherto unknown.
William Wordsworth, poet

BITE THE WAX TADPOLE

When Coca-Cola first entered the Chinese market in 1928, company representatives faced the conundrum of coming up with a sequence of characters that represented the sounds 'koh ka ko lah' without meaning anything ridiculous or obscene. While they deliberated, local shopkeepers devised their own solutions, anxious to capitalise on demand for the fizzy black elixir. They had at their disposal some 200 characters capable of representing the requisite syllables. The most felicitous and therefore widely used permutations literally meant 'Bite the wax tadpole' and 'Wax-flattened mare'. Neither sent quite the right message back to Atlanta. So the marketing team was forced to compromise. Eventually, by substituting the sound 'ler' for the more ambitious 'lah', they hit on a sentence pronounced roughly as desired that also made some kind of sense. The official character representation of the most famous brand name on Earth now translates as 'Let the mouth rejoice!'

Lest Pepsi be tempted to snigger, the company should remember its own marketing tribulations in the Far East. 'Bring your ancestors back to life with Pepsi!', one Taiwanese campaign inadvertently exhorted.

TRADEMARKS IN THE MEDIEVAL AND RENAISSANCE WORLDS

Twelfth century – Trade guilds begin to use distinguishing marks.

Thirteenth century – Bell makers start using marks. Watermarks first appear in Italy.

1266 – Earliest English law on trademarks: The Bakers Marking Law. Some bakers stamp a mark on the bread, others prick it.

1353 – Statute passed enabling merchants whose goods had been pirated to provide evidence of ownership using marks.

1365 – The Cutlers obtain protection for their monopoly and their marks in London, requiring registration with city officials.

1373 – Bottle-makers are required to place a mark on bottles and other vessels for identification purposes.

1452 – Earliest known trademark litigation: A widow is granted the use of her husband's mark.

1618 – First recorded case of trademark infringement (Southern v. How). A cloth manufacturer is found guilty of appropriating the mark of another clothier and using it on lower quality material.

A CRYPTIC INVENTOR

Who is this?
CDAVI
Answer on page 153.

UNCLONABLE STRIPES

In late 2001, cat lovers everywhere rejoiced at the birth of the world's first feline clone. But when Genetic Savings and Clone (GSC), in conjunction with Texas A&M University, unveiled the long awaited kitten, observers couldn't help noticing that she was singularly unlike her 'donor'. Rainbow was an aloof calico cat with gold, black and tan markings, whereas CC (alternatively interpreted as 'Carbon Copy' or 'Copy Cat') was a playful animal with grey tiger stripes.

'Calicos happen to have a genetic anomaly that prevents the replication of their specific coloration and markings pattern through the cloning process,' explained a GSC representative. It also seems that in all breeds, the exact position of the clone in the uterus determines which hair follicles are invaded by colour-producing cells.

GSC will clone your pet for US$50,000, but expects the figure to half in the near future. The company also offers a gene-banking service for US$895 plus an annual maintenance fee of US$100. But whatever the genes say, it won't be Tiddles.

Nervy Betty, the abandoned mascot of the Bondex basement wall sealant business, was a living parable of the dangers of putting off essential DIY. As her home crumbles about her, all she can do is sit paralysed with terror, gnawing her fingernails and staring into space. For God's sake do something woman!

The Bondex line was 'absorbed' by DAP in 1999

Image from The Orphanage of Cast-Off Mascots, www.lileks.com/institute/orphanage

FOOTBALLERS AND INTELLECTUAL PROPERTY

During the early days of Paul Gascoigne's illustrious soccer career, it had yet to register with some members of the British legal profession that the player was widely known as 'Gazza'. 'Isn't that a Rossini opera?' one judge remarked when confronted by the word in court. 'Ah yes, I know, *La Gazza Ladra* – *The Thieving Magpie*!' But after Gascoigne won the nation's hearts by bursting into tears during the 1990 World Cup semi-final against West Germany, there was little danger of the mistake being repeated. Gazza-mania broke out, and the player's representatives shrewdly registered the nickname as a trademark. The registration covered everything from soaps and perfumes to CDs and medallions.

In 1997, it was reported that Gascoigne's lawyers had threatened the soft drink manufacturer Britvic with legal action for using the phrase 'You can't beat a Red Card, Gazza' to market its Red Card energy drink. By this stage, however, Gascoigne's earlier registrations appeared to have lapsed.

Though I have no objection to Peche Melba, I have the strongest objection to my name being calmly taken for any object which the proprietor considers suitable, from scent to hairpins. America is particularly prone to this sort of piracy. I was wandering down a street in New York one day, when I suddenly stopped short before an immense drug store, across the windows of which were splashed advertisements for Melba perfume. 'Ah,' I thought, 'I think I deserve a bottle of this.' So I went inside. I said, 'May I smell the perfume Melba?' 'Certainly,' said the assistant, and sprayed some on my wrist. One sniff was enough. I hated the stuff. Then, I humbly asked who had given them the permission to call this 'creation' Melba. 'Oh, that's all right,' drawled the assistant. 'We found out her name is Mrs Armstrong and we've just as much right to call this stuff Melba as she has'.

Dame Nellie Melba, *Melodies and Memories*

QUOTE UNQUOTE

This is the patent age of new inventions
For killing bodies, and for saving souls,
All propagated with the best intentions.
Lord Byron, *Don Juan*, Canto 1, stanza 132

IRONICALLY...

The Walt Disney Company was the major lobbyist behind Sonny Bono's Copyright Term Extension Act, which extended the standard protection in the US to 95 years. It has also made extensive use of out-of-copyright material, some of which would have been unavailable to it on its own terms had they applied at the time:

1 *Fantasia* (1940) – Several pieces of classical music used in the film were out of copyright at the time but would not have been under the 95-year rule.
2 *Pinocchio* (1940) – Carlo Collodi's book was first published in 1880.
3 *Song of the South* (1946) – based on the Uncle Remus stories written by Joe Chandler Harris (c.1845–1908).
4 *Alice in Wonderland* (1951) – Lewis Caroll's classic children's novel was published in 1864.
5 *The Jungle Book* (1967) – Kipling's novel was published in 1894.

To be fair, we should point out that Disney has also made many films based on books subject to copyright at the time, such as *Peter Pan* (1953), and the company has naturally paid for the privilege.

'With this prelude, Mr Meagles went through the narrative; the established narrative, which has become tiresome; the matter-of-course narrative which we all know by heart. How, after interminable attendance and correspondence, after infinite impertinences, ignorances, and insults, my lords made a Minute, number three thousand four hundred and seventy-two, allowing the culprit to make certain trials of his invention at his own expense.

How the trials were made in the presence of a board of six, of whom two ancient members were too blind to see it, two other ancient members were too deaf to hear it, one other ancient member was too lame to get near it, and the final ancient member was too pigheaded to look at it. How there were more years; more impertinences, ignorances, and insults. How my lords then made a Minute, number five thousand one hundred and three, whereby they resigned the business to the Circumlocution Office*. How the Circumlocution Office, in course of time, took up the business as if it were a brand new thing of yesterday, which had never been heard of before; muddled the business, addled the business, tossed the business in a wet blanket. How the impertinences, ignorances, and insults went through the multiplication table. How there was a reference of the invention to three Barnacles and a Stilt-stalking, who knew nothing about it; into whose heads nothing could be hammered about it; who got bored about it, and reported physical impossibilities about it. How the Circumlocution Office, in a Minute, number eight thousand seven hundred and forty, 'saw no reason to reverse the decision at which my lords had arrived.' How the Circumlocution Office, being reminded that my lords had arrived at no decision, shelved the business. How there had been a final interview with the head of the Circumlocution Office that very morning, and how the Brazen Head had spoken, and had been, upon the whole, and under all the circumstances, and looking at it from the various points of view, of opinion that one of two courses was to be pursued in respect of the business: that was to say, either to leave it alone for evermore, or to begin it all over again.'

* *'The Circumlocution Office' is Dickens's sarcastic name for the Patent Office.*

Charles Dickens, *Little Dorrit*

GOING TO THE DOGS

Ireland's first patent, issued in 1929, was for a starter cage for greyhounds and racing breeds of that ilk. Some wags commented that the country was going to the dogs.

COCA-COLA SLOGANS: THE LAST 60 YEARS

1948	Where There's Coke There's Hospitality
1949	Along the Highway to Anywhere
1952	What You Want Is a Coke
1956	Coca-Cola...Makes Good Things Taste Better
1957	Sign of Good Taste
1958	The Cold, Crisp Taste of Coke
1959	Be Really Refreshed
1963	Things Go Better with Coke
1969	It's the Real Thing
1971	I'd Like to Buy the World a Coke
1975	Look Up America
1976	Coke Adds Life
1979	Have a Coke and a Smile
1982	Coke Is It!
1985	We've Got a Taste for You
1985	America's Real Choice
1986	Red, White & You
1987	When Coca-Cola is Part of Your Life, You Can't Beat the Feeling
1988	You Can't Beat the Feeling
1989	Official Soft Drink of the Summer
1990	You Can't Beat the Real Thing
1993	Always Coca-Cola
2000	Coca-Cola. Enjoy
2001	Life Tastes Good

BIKRAM CHOUDHURY: THE GUY'S GOT BALLS

Around the year 2000, yoga teachers across America received letters from Bikram Choudhury – inventor of Bikram yoga and founder of Bikram's Yoga College of India – warning them to copy his methods at their peril. They were informed that his exercise sequence, involving the performance of 26 exercises in a mirrored room heated to precisely 41°C, was thoroughly protected by intellectual property law. (In fact he was jumping the gun. Choudhury finally obtained federal copyright registration for his sequence in 2003, but not for the postures themselves, which he freely admitted were some 5,000 years old). Any lingering doubts about Choudhury's seriousness were dispelled by an interview he gave to a national magazine shortly afterwards. 'I have balls like atom bombs, two of them, 100-megatons each,' the Yogi announced.

WE'RE NOT NAMED AFTER A FRUIT, YOU IDIOT, IT'S A WEIRD FLIGHTLESS BIRD!

Back in the early twentieth century, a succulent, tart, green-fleshed fruit was still growing wild in the forests and scrublands of China and Siberia. It was known locally as 'Yang Tao', to foreigners as the Chinese Gooseberry and to botanists as *Actinidia deliciosa*. In 1904, a New Zealander named Katie Frazer brought some Yang Tao back to her home in Wanganui, where they thrived in the temperate conditions.

During the 1960s, New Zealand farmers started to market the fruit globally under the name kiwifruit, hoping to forge an association between their country and high quality Chinese Gooseberries. The ploy worked extremely well – almost too well for some New Zealanders, who grew tired of foreigners assuming that their national nickname was derived from the fruit rather than vice-versa. By the late 1970s, the kiwifruit was earning New Zealand hundreds of millions of dollars per annum. But the exporters made a dreadful mistake: they failed to trademark the name.

By the following decade, the majority of the world's kiwifruit were being grown outside their adopted country. In an effort to recapture lost ground, the New Zealand growers renamed the local version of the fruit the Zespri, and this time remembered to submit a trademark application. They also worked on the development of new, name-protected varieties such as the hairless, yellow Zespri Gold. But some believe that the damage will only really be undone when New Zealanders start being described as 'zespris'.

TOP 10 FIRMS BY NUMBER OF INTERNATIONAL PCT PATENT APPLICATIONS

Koninklijke Philips Electronics NV
Siemens Aktiengesellschaft
Robert Bosch GmbH
Telefonaktiebolaget LM Ericsson
Matsushita Electric Industrial Co. Ltd.
Sony Corporation
Nokia Corporation
3M Innovative Properties Company
Bayer Aktiengesellschaft
Procter & Gamble

PCT = filed under the Patent Cooperation Treaty

Source: WIPO (2002)

CELEBRITY INVENTORS

Julie Newmar

Julie Newmar played the slightly kinky catwoman in the original Batman series. She was back in the public eye in 1995 when her name was mentioned in the title of the film *To Wong Foo, Thanks for Everything, Julie Newmar*. But she should be equally well remembered for her invention of the 'Cheeky Derriere' pantyhose, a garment providing a 'balloon look for the buttocks'.

Her patent application (dated 18 January 1977) explains more about this much-needed device:

'The present invention provides pantyhose of a resilient stretch-able fabric which enhance the natural shape of a wearer's derriere giving it cheeky relief, rather than board-like flatness. The pantyhose include a rear panty portion which covers and confines the wearer's buttocks. An elastic shaping band is attached to the rear panty portion and is connected from the vicinity of the wearer's crotch zone rearward to the vicinity of a waist band of the pantyhose. The elastic shaping band fits between the wearer's buttocks to produce the desired cheeky relief thereof.'

SO THAT'S WHO HE REMINDED US OF...

In 2003, it was reported that a Russian law firm had been instructed to commence proceedings against Warner Brothers for using President Vladimir Putin as the model for the character of Dobby the house-elf in *Harry Potter and the Chamber of Secrets*. This was difficult to confirm, as both parties declined to comment, but many Russians assumed the story to be true. Ever since, Harry Potter websites and chatrooms have been bombarded with angry messages.

JUST ONE CORNETTO, GIVE IT TO ME . . .

When the famously foul-mouthed British Chef, Gordon Ramsay, dished up a new pudding known as the 'home-made mini-cornetto' in one of his London restaurants, it didn't take long for Unilever, the real makers of Cornetto, to take notice. Unilever lawyers warned Ramsay, star of the celebrity cook-up programme *Hell's Kitchen*, to remove the item from his menu, as it was likely to 'damage the distinctiveness of our Cornetto mark. Ramsay was reportedly reluctant to agree, remarking 'If anything we are improving the image of Cornetto in giving it a new twist'.

In the summer of 2004, a Unilever spokesman revealed that the company had 'received a telephone call from the restaurant apologising and stating that they had removed the name from their menu and website.'

Shortly after moving from Blackburn Rovers to Newcastle United for a world record £15 million transfer fee in August 1996, Alan Shearer decided to trademark his face (UK Trademark No. 2117215). It therefore became illegal to use the former England striker's image on items ranging from sunglasses to umbrellas without his permission. The renewal date is 30 November 2006.

The first draft of this item jocularly suggested that Shearer might also wish to consider trademarking his nonchalant arm-aloft-with-flat-palm goal celebration. It transpired that this had already been done, with the player's consent, by an unemployed tiler from Hexham in Northumberland. Colin Walton, a life-long Newcastle fan, had visions of a range of T-shirts depicting the Magpie's number 9 performing the salute above the legend 'Shear We Go!' Finding that neither the image nor the slogan were trademarked, Walton obtained the blessing of both the club and the player's management team before proceeding with the registration. As a sweetener, he agreed to donate 10% of earnings from shirt sales to Shearer's favourite charity, the NSPCC.

For the record, you'd better not use his image if you're in the business of:

Class 09: Teaching, training and instructional films, videos and cassette tapes; computer programmes; sun glasses and spectacles.

Class 16: Instructional and teaching materials; photographs, posters and cartoons; printed matter; magazines, periodicals and books; pens and pencils.

Class 18: Bags, holdalls, haversacks, rucksacks, backpacks, luggage, trunks and suitcases; purses and wallets; briefcases; umbrellas.

Class 25: Articles of clothing; footwear; headgear.

Class 28: Sporting and gymnastic articles; sports training apparatus; and parts and fittings for all the aforesaid goods; balls.

ATOMIC GOLF BALLS

In the early days of atomic energy, the BF Goodrich Company, better known for its tyres, developed a prototype atomic golf ball. The idea was that the radioactive core would be easy to locate with a Geiger counter, facilitating the task of finding the ball if it landed in the rough.

Eventually the company decided the invention was unworkable. It was probably for the best.

Registered US trademark of G&S Restaurant Services (published for opposition August 2004)

SOME SURPRISING SAMPLES

SAMPLER	SAMPLEE

SAMPLER
The Beastie Boys *Hey Ladies*
(macho white rappers adopt glam tune)

SAMPLEE
The Sweet *Ballroom Blitz*

Pras, Mya and ODB
Ghetto Supastar
(putting the country back into the urban jungle)

Kenny Rogers and Dolly Parton
Islands in the Stream

Shaggy *Angel*
('Boombastic' reggae artist borrows from 1973 rock classic. Had there been a copyright issue, he'd doubtless have said 'It Wasn't Me')

Steve Miller Band *The Joker*

Notorious B.I.G.
Been Around the World
(murdered New York hip hop star meets down to earth Rochdale chick)

Lisa Stansfield
All Around the World

Eminem *Stan*
(foul mouthed rapper hooks up with 'butter wouldn't melt' ex-Westminster girl)

Dido *Thank You*

Sonic Youth *Into the Groovy*
(Moody experimentalist band turn Madge's bubbly hit thoroughly malevolent)

Madonna *Into the Groove*

Oasis *Hello*
(Manchester rockers pay homage to... no, let's not go there)

Garry Glitter *Hello Hello*

QUOTE UNQUOTE

Only one thing is impossible for God; to find any sense in any copyright law on the planet.
Mark Twain, US writer

I KNEW THERE WAS SOMETHING WRONG WITH THEM...

This is the biggest thing since sliced bread – the straight banana. Depending on the degree of the curve, chunks will be cut out of the banana, which are then resealed using a biologically safe plaster... I believe the straight cigar-banana will drive the curved banana from the market. It's easier to eat, and easier to store.
German Artist Karl-Friederich Lentze, October 2004, on his patent application for an urgently needed banana-straightening device.

Position of the CD in the 'Top 100 Inventions of All Time' as 67
voted by visitors to scenta.co.uk in 2004

WHY LITERACY IS STILL IMPORTANT
IN THE COMPUTER AGE

In February 2004, John Zuccarini of Hollywood, Florida, became the first person successfully prosecuted under the recently-enacted 'Amber Alert' law. This is a federal statute making it a crime to lure children onto adult websites sites, a practice known as 'mousetrapping'. Zuccarini's technique had been to register misspelled versions of websites likely to be appeal to kids. When these sites were visited (a frequent occurrence given youthful spelling habits), the unwitting surfer would be redirected to a site advertising pornography, instant credit, gambling and other inappropriate stuff. Because each visit was deemed a 'hit' in advertising terms, Zuccarini was thought to have been earning around $1 million a year through the scam. He was sentenced to two and a half years' imprisonment.

A JUMBLED INVENTOR

Unscramble the anagram:
'Simon the saddo'
Answer on page 153.

SIX RIDICULOUSLY SHORT DOMAIN NAMES

p.ro (no need for 'www') • 3.am (ditto)
ns.nl (ditto) • www.com
www.ru • www.kz

NATIONAL INVENTIVE SURGES

In 2002, the countries showing the greatest increase in number of patent applications year on year under the Patent Cooperation Treaty included:

India – 51.9%
Netherlands – 26.1%
Switzerland – 22.8%
Mexico – 19.6%
Singapore – 18.8%
Japan – 14.2%
Germany – 12.1%
USA – 11.5%
South Korea – 10.1%

Applications from developing nations were noted to have risen by 700% since 1997.

The alarm clock was invented in 1787 by Levi Hutchins of Concord, New Hampshire. It was fairly useless however: the clock only rang at 4am.

THE GREAT INVENTORS

Donald Duncan

Although DF Duncan Senior, born 1892, was a talented inventor (he co-patented a four-wheel hydraulic car brake and came up with the Eskimo Pie), his real genius was marketing. He was, for example, the brains behind the first premium incentive ('send in two cereal packet lids and we'll send you a free x, y or z'), and largely responsible for the inexorable spread of the parking meter.

The product most closely associated with Duncan, however, was already several thousand years old when he adopted it. The yo-yo had been a favourite toy of the Ancient Greeks, and the Filipinos had been using spiked versions for hunting and fighting for hundreds of years (they had 20-foot strings). Indeed, the word 'yo-yo' comes to us from Tagalog, the native language of the Philippines. But they were completely unfamiliar to Americans when Pedro Flores, a Filipino immigrant, started manufacturing them in California during the 1920s.

When Duncan saw the toy, he sprang into action. In 1929, he bought the rights from Flores for $25,000, trademarked the name Yo-Yo and improved the design, introducing a sliding loop around the axle instead of a knot. Then teams of salesmen were dispatched around the country to seduce the public with demonstrations of tricks like 'walking the dog' and 'around the world'. Duncan also struck a deal with William Randolph Hearst to get free advertising. In return, he organised a series of yo-yo competitions in which subscription to Heart's newspapers was an entry requirement.

The campaign was phenomenally successful. Duncan's factory in Luck, Wisconsin was soon churning out 3,600 yo-yos every hour. In one month in 1931, three million of the toys were sold just in Philadelphia. Sales peaked at 45 million units in 1962, but paradoxically, this was the point at which production and advertising costs spiralled out of control. Duncan was forced to sell, and the Flambeau Plastic Co acquired the company name and trademarks.

Duncan died in 1971. Had he lived for 21 more years, he would have seen the ancient toy he had re-popularised launched into space aboard the Shuttle Atlantis.

THE NUMBERS 1 TO 10 AS US TRADEMARKS

You can't copyright or patent a number*, thank heavens, or we'd all be in serious trouble. But you can trademark it, or at least its rendition in the manner specified in the official documentation.

To qualify for the list, a product or service's officially registered word mark must consist only of the digit(s) in question.

1 – Trademarked by (among many others) Ashland Inc, Kentucky, manufacturers of automobile wheel cleaners.

2 – Owned by Vector Tobacco Ltd of Bermuda. Denotes a brand of cigarettes.

3 – Registered as a trademark by The Royal Patel Corp, North Carolina, for a real estate operation (Vector Tobacco have also bagged this one for one of their cigarette brands).

4 – A registered trademark of Swingline staplers.

5 – Chanel, as in what Marilyn Monroe claimed to wear in bed.

6 – Registered to the Neuf Company, Paris, for a range of bags, perfumes and cosmetics.

7 – A brand of whiskey owned by Diageo.

8 – A trademarked line of clothing, TM owned by Elttab G4B Ltd of Florida.

9 – A business marketing and consulting service owned by Peacock Nine Ltd of Chicago.

10 – Trademark of a range of car lighting products made by Truck-Lite Co, Inc of Falconer, New York.

* Some logarithms used in computing are exceptions to the rule, but let's not worry about them.

MUSIC LESSONS

Such is the problem of illegally downloaded music, children are now being taught about music piracy and copyright issues in the classroom. The problems of music piracy cost the UK music industry millions of pounds every year and, as elsewhere in the world, is also blamed for the decline in the sales of CDs. But in 2003, the board of British Music Rights – a British trade organisation promoting the interests of composers, songwriters and music publishers – decided to do something about it. They worked with education experts to put together a learning pack aimed at 11 to 14-year-old school children. A case of less lessons in doh-ray-me and more in don't-touch-Napster.

70 *Number of years after the death of the author that copyright protection expires in the USA and the EC*

Long before it occurred to anyone to use this design for church roofs and castle battlements, King Athelwolf employed it in his Stay-Dry Crown.

QUOTE UNQUOTE

Name the greatest of all the inventors. Accident.
Mark Twain, US writer

'PEPSI JOAN'

Coca-Cola may have been endorsed by some big names, but none was as dedicated as the actress Joan Crawford was to the company's greatest rival. From 1955 to 1973 she worked as a publicity executive for Pepsi, and in 1959 she took her fourth husband's place on the board following his death. He had been Alfred Steele, the president of the company.

Crawford's crowning achievement at Pepsi was winning the Sixth Annual 'Pally' Award, for the employee contributing most to company sales. Thereafter, she displayed the bronze Pepsi bottle next to the Oscar she had won for her role in Mildred Pierce.

GLOBES IN THE AIR

Although the Montgolfier brothers are rightly credited with the invention of the hot air balloon, the version used for the first demonstration of the new technology in Paris was designed by a rival scientist (Jacques Charles) and filled with hydrogen. When the unmanned gas balloon landed near Gonesse, just outside the capital, on 27 August 1783, the terrified villagers assumed it was something demonic and set upon it with pitchforks. Anticipating this kind of reaction, the French government had issued the following proclamation to quell public anxiety:

Announcement to the People on the Ascent of Balloons or Globes in the Air
A discovery has been made, which the Government deems it right to be made known, so that alarm be not occasioned to the people.

On calculating the different weights of inflammable and common air, it has been found that a balloon filled with inflammable air* will rise towards heaven until it is in equilibrium with the surrounding air. This may not happen until it has reached a great height.

The first experiment was made at Annonay in Vivrais by the inventors Messieurs Montgolfier; a globe formed of canvas and paper, 105 feet in circumference, filled with inflammable air**, reached an uncalculated height.

The same experiment has just been repeated in Paris (27 August at 5pm) in the presence of a great crowd. A globe of taffeta, covered by elastic gum, 36 feet in circumference, has risen from the Champs de Mars, and been lost to view in the clouds, being borne in a north-easterly direction; it is impossible to foresee where it will descend.

It is proposed to repeat these experiments on a larger scale. Anyone who sees such a globe (which resembles a darkened moon) in the sky should be aware that, far from being an alarming phenomenon, it is only a machine, made of taffeta, or light canvas covered in paper, which cannot possibly cause any harm and which will some day prove serviceable to the wants of society

* hydrogen.

** the authorities get it wrong here. The Montgolfier balloon had been powered by hot air.

MR POTATO HEAD

Mr Potato Head was invented and patented by George Lerner of New York City in 1952 and subsequently sold to Hasbro Inc, which continues to manufacture him. 'MPH' has played a surprisingly active role in American history. The first toy advertised on television, in 1984, he also managed to win four votes in the mayoral election in Boise, Idaho.

COVERING UP

The leotard came into existence in the 1880s. It was named after a young French acrobat called Jules Léotard, who invented the flying trapeze act by stringing some swings over his father's swimming pool. Léotard performed in a tight, self-designed one-piece costume. Unsurprisingly, his scantily dressed flying act was immensely popular with the tightly-corseted young ladies of Victorian England. His notoriety as a lover was sealed when George Leybourne wrote a hit music hall song entitled *The Daring Young Man on the Flying Trapeze*:

> *Oh, he floats through the air*
> *With the greatest of ease,*
> *This daring young man*
> *On the flying trapeze;*
> *His actions are graceful,*
> *All girls he does please,*
> *My love he has purloined away!*

Sadly, reality failed to live up to the legend. Jules died at the tender age of 30, probably from smallpox, just as the term 'leotard' was gaining popular currency. Had he been alive to trademark his scandalous gym wear, he might well have ended up swinging from the rooftops of the largest banks in Europe.

FRUITIEST PERFUME FORMULA

Calvin Klein's *Escape* contains:
1. apple
2. blackcurrant
3. litchi
4. mandarin
5. peach
6. plum

BUT THAT'S MY REAL NAME!

In November 2003, a Canadian teenager named Mike Rowe (founder of a business called mikerowesoft.com) received a letter from Microsoft lawyers accusing him of copyright infringement and demanding immediate transfer of his domain name to the company. Rowe requested a monetary settlement to cover his time and expenses. Microsoft's initial counter-offer? US$10. Beseiged by bad publicity, the company later helped Rowe set up a new business, paid for his Microsoft Certification training, and gave him an Xbox game system.

THE ROOTS OF PUNK ROCK

Walter Hunt was extremely creative, but a lousy businessman. In 1834, for example, he invented America's first sewing machine, but elected not to patent it for fear of putting hand-sewers out of work. Twenty years later, Elias Howe came up with a similar machine, patented it, and cleaned up.

Hunt's most famous invention came about in 1849. One day, while worrying about a US$15 debt to a friend, he started fiddling with a piece of brass wire. A few twists and coils later, Hunt realised he had a cheap, simple fastening device in his hands – the world's first safety pin. He took out a patent on his creation (US Patent No. 6,281) and sold the rights for US$400. Thus he was able to pay his friend back but lost out on millions.

QUOTE UNQUOTE

That secular cloister where I hatched my most beautiful ideas and where we had such good times together.
Albert Einstein, in a nostalgic letter to a former colleague at the Berne Patent Office, where he worked between 1901 and 1908

8 FICTIONAL INVENTORS

Doc Brown from *Back to the Future*
'Dad' from *Honey I Shrunk the Kids*
Q in the James Bond novels and films
Professor Calculus from the Tintin books
Inspector Gadget
Dr Frankenstein
Captain Nemo
Willy Wonka

BABY GAYS

Q-Tip Cotton Swabs were originally known as 'Baby Gays'. They were invented by Leo Gerstenzang, a Polish American who had served in the US Army during World War One. In 1922, Gerstenzang and his wife started the Leo Gerstenzang Infant Novelty Company, which made baby care products. Having noticed his wife wrapping wads of cotton around toothpicks when bathing their baby daughter, Gerstenzang decided to develop a machine to manufacture similar swabs, 'untouched by human hands'.

Q-Tips was registered as a trademark by Q-Tips Inc in 1957. The brand is now owned by Chesebrough-Pond's Inc.

SPOT THE DIFFERENCE

Can you identify the differences between these two song lyrics?

Jesus in a camper van/He said sorry to leave you but I've done all I can/I suppose even the Son of God gets it hard sometimes/Especially when he goes round saying I am the way
(from *Jesus in a Camper Van* by Robbie Williams)

Every Son of God gets a little hard luck some time/Every Son of God gets a little hard luck some time/Every Son Of God gets a little hard luck some time/ Especially when He goes round saying He's the way.
(from *I am the Way* by Loudon Wainwright III)

In October 2000, the High Court deemed that there weren't enough of them. Williams and his co-songwriter Guy Chambers were found guilty of 'substantially' appropriating lyrics from Wainwright's own reworking of the Woodie Guthrie song, *I am the Way*. In a further development, Mr Justice Pumphrey refused to award punitive damages against the defendants in 2002 on the grounds that the infringement was neither cynical nor flagrant. He also professed 'grave doubts as to who has actually won this case'. The idea for the song came to Robbie during a spell in rehab.

A NARA ESCAPE

In May 2004, Japanese priests from the Tadaiji Temple in the ancient city of Nara intervened to prevent a local company registering the name 'Snot from the nose of the Great Buddha' as a trademark. Yamamoto Bussan had been marketing the candy for three years in a packet adorned with a cartoon of the Enlightened One picking his nose.

AQUARIAN PIONEERS

The general consensus among astrologers is that children born under the sign of Aquarius have the best chances of growing up to be successful inventors and innovators. Here are some Aquarians who offer supporting evidence:

Charles Darwin (February 12, 1809) – evolutionist
Thomas Alva Edison (February 11, 1847) – inventor
Charles Lindberg (February 2, 1902) – pilot
Wolfgang Mozart (January 27, 1766) – composer
Edwin 'Buzz' Aldrin (January 20, 1930) – astronaut
Alfred Adler (February 7, 1870) – psychiatrist
Jules Verne (February 8, 1828) – French sci-fi writer and visionary

SOME IP-RELATED ACRONYMS

AIPA: American Inventors Protection Act of 1999

AIPLA: American Intellectual Property Law Association

AMPICTA: Australian Manufacturers, Patents, Industrial Designs, Copyright and Trade Marks Association

CIPO: Canadian Intellectual Property Office

CTM: Community Trade Mark

CTMO: Community Trade Mark Office

CTMR: Community Trade Mark Regulation

DNRC: Domain Names Rights Coalition

EAST: Examiners Automated Search System

EPO: European Patent Office

IACC: International Anti-Counterfeiting Coalition

INTA: International Trademark Association

IPO: Intellectual Property Owners Association

JPO: Japan Patent Office

OAPI: Organisation Africaine de la Propriété Intellectuelle (African Intellectual Property Organisation)

NIPLECC: National Intellectual Property Law Enforcement Coordination Council

PAIR: Patent Application Information Retrieval system

PALM: Patent Application Location and Monitoring system

PCT: Patent Cooperation Treaty

PLT: Patent Law Treaty

PPAC: Patent Public Advisory Committee

TARR: Trademark Application Registration Retrieval system

TCT: Trademark Cooperation Treaty

TEAS: Trademark Electronic Application System

TESS: Trademark Electronic Search System

TRAM: Trademark Reporting and Monitoring system

TRIP: Trade Related Aspects of Intellectual Property

UPR: Utility, Plant and Reissue applications

WCT: WIPO Copyright Treaty

WIPO: World Intellectual Property Organization

WPPT: WIPO Performances and Phonograms Treaty

A HAPPY HOME

On 1 December 1999, the Texan entrepreneur Mark Ostrofsky netted a world record US$7.5 million from the sale of the domain name business.com. The family nanny, however, went a few steps better. During the same week, three years earlier, that he had originally purchased the rights from a London-based Internet Service Provider for US$150,000, she had scooped US$21 million on the Texas State Lottery.

Mr Ostrofsky's wife also has luck on her side. Every month she receives a dozen roses from eflowers.com, in line with a condition laid down by her husband when he sold the domain name to the company for US$25,000.

76 *Total number of trademarks registered internationally under the Madrid Agreement in 1893*

CATTLE BRANDS

Some of the first trademarks to be used in America were cattle brands.

Spanish Brand Marks granted by the King of Spain:

Don Juan Joseph Flores
Granted July 1, 1762

Provincial Company,
Rio Grande, circa 1817

Recorded in Nagadoches
May 5, 1828

Brands from Austin, Texas:

Simon Green
Austin, Texas

GS Jones
Austin, Texas

A Bahn
Austin, Texas

Brands Using Animal Imagery:

Sorell Smith
San Saba, Texas

CS Pix
1857

EP Moorehead
Del Rio, Texas

With thanks to: Austin Library, University of Texas

INTELLECTUAL PROPERTY PARADOXES

The vast majority of software patents are never used. Instead, they are accumulated by large corporations to ward off competition. Or they are held by individuals or companies who are intimidated by the possibility of litigation, and hence too afraid to use them. The situation has been described as a corporate version of Mutually Assured Destruction (MAD), the 'if anyone makes a move we'll all get nuked' doctrine that sustained an uneasy peace during the Cold War.

10 MOST EXPENSIVE DOMAIN NAMES IN 2004

According to DNJournal.com, the most lucrative domain name sales during the first two thirds of 2004 were:

creditcards.com	US$2.5 million
mercury.com	US$700,000
ME.com	US$460,000
smoking.com	US$325,000
arab.com	US$225,000
visitflorida.com	US$186,000
commerce.com	US$180,000
beef.com	US$50,000
IQtest.de	EUR123,650
TourismAustralia.com	AUS$201,000

THE PUREST FORM OF PLAGIARISM

Staff at Stanford University were somewhat taken aback when they discovered that their teaching assistant's handbook section on plagiarism cropped up in a similar handbook put out by the University of Oregon. Oregon officials conceded that the section, and indeed other parts of its handbook, were identical with the Stanford guidebook, promptly apologised and revised their text.

Who said irony was dead?

THE MOST FREQUENTLY REPRODUCED
IMAGES IN THE WORLD

1. Mickey Mouse – *featured on more than
7,500 products at the last count.*
2. Jesus Christ
3. Elvis Presley

This makes a mockery of John Lennon's famous remark about the Beatles being more popular than Jesus.

THE KING AND INTELLECTUAL PROPERTY

His Majesty King Bhumibol Adulyadej of Thailand is a man of many talents. An accomplished jazz saxophonist and enthusiastic radio ham, he is also, at the time of writing, the holder of four Thai patents.

The first and second were awarded for a contraption for oxygenating polluted water, a major health hazard within Thailand. During the 1980s, the King had addressed the problem by promoting the use of two simple techniques: 'good water chases bad water', which diverted fresh water to dilute tainted supplies, and 'evil overcomes evil', where water hyacinth and assorted aquatic plants were grown to filter waste. But neither was a match for the Chaipattana Low Speed Surface Aerator. Loosely based on a traditional luk or water-wheel, the device won King Bhumibol the 'Best Inventor' award at the prestigious Brussels Eureka show in 2000. According to an official website, the King, concerned about his subjects' lackadaisical attitude to intellectual property registration, decided to patent the aerator to provide them with a positive example.

His Majesty's third patent is for a cost-saving fuel based on a combination of regular diesel and palm oil. Unlike ethanol-based alternatives, the fluid can be used in trucks and other machines without their engines requiring modification. The monarch's formula was expected to save the country hundreds of millions of baht per annum.

The fourth patent is the fruit of the King's most grandiose project to date: cracking the age-old puzzle of how to control the weather. His 'super-sandwich' rain-making technique relies on aircraft simultaneously 'seeding' clouds at different altitudes/temperatures with chemicals known to trigger precipitation. King Buhmibol's technique is believed to direct rain to specific targets more efficiently than any previous rain-generating method. The 75-year-old ruler was presented with the patent at his seaside palace in Hua Hin on 2 June 2003.

A king who can rain out your picnic – no wonder his subjects treat him with reverence.

OUCH

When Dr Alan de Vibliss of Toledo, Ohio, invented the spray gun in 1803, he expected it to be used in the administration of medication to the oral and nasal passages. The idea was to reduce the need for swabs. He would no doubt be amazed to find his brainchild so central to the lives of automobile manufacturers and graffiti artists.

FOOTBALLERS (OR AT LEAST THEIR WIVES) AND INTELLECTUAL PROPERTY

The Beckhams are known to go to great lengths to control their lucrative public images, but Victoria Beckham bit off more than she could chew in 2002 when she attempted to prevent Peterborough United from registering the nickname 'Posh' as a trademark. Geoff Davey, the club's chief executive, was astonished to receive a letter from the former Spice Girl's lawyers informing him of their opposition. 'I was absolutely stunned', Davey admitted. 'One reason was that our claim to the use of the name "Posh" should be challenged. The second reason was that someone as big as Victoria Beckham would want to raise this particular challenge. The name is part of the club's history and tradition.'

Although a class-conscious pedant might question whether either party was 100% 'posh' in the technical sense, the unglamorous East Anglian soccer club certainly acquired the disputed nickname ahead of the Hertfordshire chanteuse. Peterborough United were known as 'Posh' from the moment the club was founded in 1934. They inherited the moniker from a previous local team, Peterborough and Fletton United, which folded two years earlier. Back in 1921, Peterborough and Fletton's player-manager Pat Tirrel had put word around that he was looking for 'Posh players for a Posh team', and the nickname had stuck

To explain their client's controversial move, Mrs Beckham's publicity company issued a statement: 'Whilst Victoria accepts that the football club are nicknamed Posh, and might want to use the name in association with football products, there is no conceivable reason why they should need blanket coverage for every class of goods. The name Posh is inexorably associated with Mrs Beckham in the public's mind, and the concern from her team is that they (the public) would think she had in some way endorsed products she had no knowledge of.'

Nevertheless, faced by a blizzard of bad publicity, the Beckham camp backed down. In January 2003, Geoff Davey announced that he had been led to believe that Victoria's legal team were withdrawing their objections to Peterborough's trademark registration. 'I think it's important that common sense prevails', he commented. 'There has never been an objection by Peterborough United to her use of the name.'

QUOTE UNQUOTE

We owe most of our great inventions and most of the achievements of genius to idleness – either enforced or voluntary.
Agatha Christie, British crime writer

Percentage of Christian teenagers who admitted to sharing copyrighted music in a 2004 survey

LIVE THE AD

Advertising and sponsorship have always been about using imagery to equate products with positive cultural or social experiences. What makes nineties-style branding different is that it increasingly seeks to take these associations out of the representational realm and make them a lived reality. So the goal is not merely to have child actors drinking Coke in a TV commercial, but for students to brainstorm concepts for Coke's next ad campaign in English class. It transcends logo-festooned Roots clothing designed to conjure memories of summer camp and reaches out to build an actual Roots country lodge that becomes a 3-D manifestation of the Roots brand concept. Disney transcends its sports network ESPN, a channel for guys who like to sit around in sports bars screaming at the TV, and launches a line of ESPN Sports Bars, complete with giant-screen TVs.

Naomi Klein, *No Logo*

CRYPTIC TIME

What easily overlooked area of intellectual property law does this clue embody?
Carts steered badly, giving rise to market gossip (5, 7)
Answer on page 153.

USELESS PATENTS

The 'Animal-powered Car'
You may have thought that the horse and cart went out with the invention of the internal combustion engine, but GB patent no. 2,060,081 has set out to prove you wrong. Patented in 1981, this animal-powered vehicle is propelled by a self-contained treadmill, making it not so much 'horse and cart' as 'horse in cart'.

THE HOGARTH ACT

May 1735 – The Engravers' Copyright Act receives the royal assent. It extends the regulations of the literary act ('Queen Anne's Act') of 1709 to prints, with a 14 years' copyright. The publication of *The Rake's Progress* prints was deliberately delayed until the Act took effect and appeared in August. Hogarth had been the main promoter of the campaign in favour of the new Act, which came to be referred to as Hogarth's Act. The number of pirated prints diminished rapidly. The copyright period was extended from 14 to 28 years in 1767. But Hogarth himself allowed cheaper, 'authorised' copies to be made of his own prints.

PATENT

In the beginning, 'patent' was simply an adjective meaning 'open'. It takes its root from *patens*, the present participle of the Latin verb meaning 'to be open'. The word is still used in this sense in the expression 'patently obvious'. It is also found in architecture (a 'patent' is a room allowing free passage) and botany (a 'patent plant' has widely spaced leaves or branches).

One of the term's first uses in English was the phrase 'letters patent', which denoted public proclamations issued by the monarch. Letters patent were used to bestow titles and property, and to grant exclusive licenses to individuals to manufacture or sell given products for specified time periods.

'Patent medicines', were over-the-counter remedies popular during the nineteenth century, although few of them were actually patented. Smooth, shiny 'patent leather' was once produced by a patented process, but its manufacture is now open to all.

THE COST OF COUNTERFEITING

According to a survey carried out in 1999 by the Centre for Economics and Business Research*, the annual cost in euros of counterfeiting to various sectors of the EU economy was as follows:

7.581 billion – clothing and footwear
3.017 billion – perfumes and cosmetics
3.731 billion – toys and sports equipment
1.554 billion – pharmaceuticals

For the Global Anti-Counterfeiting Group

LANDMARKS IN THE HISTORY OF GENETIC PATENTS

2000: ANDi, the first transgenic primate, is created in Oregon. The rhesus monkey had been engineered with green fluorescence-inducing jellyfish genes. The object of the exercise was to pave the way for the insertion of human genes associated with diseases such as Alzheimer's, breast cancer and diabetes into primates to learn more about how they operated. But the general public was more interested in seeing whether he would glow in the dark. (This had already been shown to be the case in similarly engineered mice). Fortunately for ANDi (whose took his name from the initials of 'inserted DNA' written backwards), he didn't. Some animals whose genes have been engineered in similar ways have not got off so lightly.

THE DAWN OF TELEVISION

In 1925 television was regarded as something of a myth. No true television had ever been shown- only crude shadows. At that time I was working very intensively in a small attic laboratory in the Soho district of London. Things were very black; my cash resources were almost exhausted, and as, day after day, success seemed as far away as ever, I began to wonder if general opinion was not, after all, correct, and television was in truth a myth. But one day, it was in fact the fifth Friday in October 1925, I experienced the one great thrill which research work has brought me. The dummy's head which I used for experimental purposes suddenly showed up on the screen, not as a mere smudge of black and white, but as a real image with details and with gradations of light and shade. I was vastly excited and ran downstairs to obtain a living object. The first person to appear was the office boy from the floor below, a youth named William Taynton, and he, rather reluctantly, consented to submit himself to the experiment. I placed him before the transmitter and went into the next room to see what the screen would show. The screen was entirely blank, and no effort of tuning would produce any result. Puzzled, and very disappointed, I went back to the transmitter, and there the cause of the failure became at once evident. The boy, scared by the intense white light had backed away from the transmitter. In the excitement of the moment I gave him half a crown (then worth 60 cents), and this time he kept his head in the right position. Going again into the next room, I saw his head on the screen quite clearly. It is curious to consider that the first person in the world to be seen by television should have required a bribe to accept that distinction.

The first transmitted apparatus... had a disc made of cardboard, and the lamp which supplied the illumination was a motor-cycle bulb enclosed in a perforated biscuit tin. The subject for all these preliminary tests was a dilapidated ventriloquist's dummy, and the whole of this conglomeration now rests in the Science Museum in London.

John Logie Baird, talking on New York City's WMCA and WCPH radio stations, 1931.

SHAMELESS PLAGIARISM

Hans Christian Andersen, of fairy tale fame, was once busted by the wife of another Danish writer lifting material verbatim from other authors for a play he was writing. 'You have copied whole paragraphs word for word from Oehlenschleger and Ingemann!' she challenged him. 'I know,' Andersen replied with a guilty grin. 'Aren't they splendid?'

*The world's first patented plant was a transgenic
cactus engineered with genetic material from
Andy Warhol's grandfather.*

QUOTE UNQUOTE

*Of all the inventions of man I doubt whether any was more easily
accomplished than that of a Heaven.*
GC Lichtenberg, German writer and physicist

GOT ELK?

When the California Milk Processing Board launched the first of its
celebrated 'Got Milk?' advertisements in 1993 and trademarked the
expression during the same year, it inadvertently sparked off a
linguistic phenomenon. Americans are now inundated with ads,
t-shirts and mail-shots enquiring whether they've 'got' just about
everything under the sun. Choice examples include 'Got Firewall?',
'Got Vote?', 'Got Water?', 'Got Jesus?' (popular as a bumper sticker),
'Got Elk?' and 'Got Parking?' (as used by the town of Castle Rock in
an official mailing).

2003 GLOBAL ANTI-COUNTERFEITING AWARDS

On June 19, 2003 ('world anti-counterfeiting day'), representatives from anti-counterfeiting organisations across the globe assembled for their industry's sixth annual awards ceremony, organised by the Global Anti-Counterfeiting Group and Authentication News. As with 'Live Aid', the event was divided between two venues, one in Washington DC and the other in Paris.

The winners and runners-up were as follows:

Public-Sector Organisation:
Winner: French Customs and Excise Service
Commended: Customs Service of Macao Special Administrative Region (People's Republic of China)
Trading Standards North-West IP Group (UK)

The French Customs and Excise Service had managed to increase its seizures of faked items from 706,729 in 1997 to 5,369,104 in 2001.

Association
Winner: Coalition for Intellectual Property Rights (Russia)
Commended: China Association of Enterprises with Foreign Investment (People's Republic of China)

CIPR is a private/public/consumer partnership formed in 1999. The Association had been instrumental in the introduction of stronger intellectual property legislation in Russia, Kazakhstan, Ukraine and Latvia.

Company
Winner: The Gillette Company
Commended: Adobe Systems France
Cartier (France)

Since 2000, Gillette had made the battle against counterfeiting a top priority, conducting hundreds of raids on manufacturers of fake razors and batteries in China and elsewhere, and generally setting a fine example to other companies.

Media
Winner: *The Economist*

The Economist had played an important role in educating readers worldwide about intellectual property. It had also struck a major blow for the industry by countering the arguments of Naomi Klein's *No Logo* in an article entitled 'Pro Logo'.

PRINCESS DI P

In October 2004, a California judge finally gave Pennsylvania-based company Franklin Mint the go-ahead to pursue a US$25 million malicious prosecution lawsuit against the Diana Princess of Wales Memorial Fund. Six years earlier, the Fund had invoked Californian Right of Publicity law in an attempt to prevent Franklin Mint selling a Princess Diana 'Limited Edition Commemorative Plate'. The court had rejected the claim, pointing out that Diana resided in a country where there were no such laws.

This had prompted Franklin Mint to counter-sue, on the grounds that the Fund's case had been 'frivolous' and therefore malicious.

What made Franklin Mint's action unusual was the company's reported pledge to donate any damages it might be awarded to charities championed by the Princess. As overlawyered.com ruefully observed, this meant that the only parties who could conceivably profit from the case were the lawyers.

CAN'T HEAR IT MYSELF,
BUT WHAT DO I KNOW?

Who was nominated for a Grammy Award in 1998
for writing the song *Bittersweet Symphony*?

(a) Richard Ashcroft of The Verve
(b) Peter Waterman of Stock Aitken & Waterman
(c) Keith Richards and Mick Jagger of The Rolling Stones

Answer on page 153.

WELL THEY DIDN'T HAVE A CALCULATOR...

In April 2001, the owners of MP3.com were ecstatic to learn that the company had been ordered to pay approximately US$300,000 in damages to record label TVT for copyright infringement. TVT had been asking for US$8.5 million, and MP3.com had been resigned to a payout in the region of 10 times the actual award. It transpired that the New York jurors had agreed a penalty of just that order, but had then written down the sum incorrectly, omitting the final zero. And one of them was a mathematics teacher.

During the ensuing weekend, the embarrassed jurors realised their error and contacted US District Judge Jed Rakoff to own up. 'This matter is far from obvious in how it should be adjudicated', he announced on his return to work.

A DEFENCE OF PLAGIARISM

Ideas improve. The meaning of words participates in the improvement. Plagiarism is necessary. Progress implies it. It embraces an author's phrase, makes use of his expressions, erases a false idea, and replaces it with the right idea.

Guy Debord, *The Society of the Spectacle*

THE MOST CREATIVE AMERICAN CITIES?

If the number of design patents issued per annum per 100,000 population is anything to go by, the following were the most creative metropolitan areas in the USA as of 1998:

Metro Area	Design pats granted	Population (in 1998)	Pats per 100,000
Sheboygan, WI	43	110,170	39.0
Portland-Vancouver, OR/WA	309	1,818,955	17.0
Akron, OH	90	688,952	13.1
San Francisco, CA	168	1,683,309	10.0
New Haven etc, CT	162	1,631,866	9.9
Orange County, CA	266	2,721,701	9.8
Boulder-Longemont, CO	26	267,274	9.7
Racine, WI	17	186,119	9.1
Minneapolis-St Paul, MN/WI	251	2,831,234	8.9

Source: United States Patent and Trademark Office

ANTI-PIRACY TECHNIQUES
IN THE SILENT FILM ERA

Piracy was a serious issue in the early days of the silent movie. Unscrupulous film companies would regularly steal a movie, replace a scene or two with newly shot material and release it as a brand new production.

The Biograph Company devised a crafty solution to the problem. It started to ensure that its trademark, the initial's 'AB', appeared somewhere in every shot. Doors, walls and windows were all fair game. Buffs can have a great time trying to spot the 'ABs' in old Biograph movies, an activity comparable to searching for the director's inevitable cameo appearance in a Hitchcock film. The device was first used on a portable gipsy piano in *Her First Adventure* (1908).

Every form to which the hands of the artist have ever given birth spring from... a natural faculty which belongs not to the artist exclusively but to Man.
George Bancroft, historian

PROTECTING YOUR GEMS

In the old days, gem cutters relied on trade secrets to prevent others copying their work. But with the pirates steadily improving their reverse-engineering skills, jewellers have increasingly been seeking intellectual property protection. Under US law, there are three main routes open to them:

Copyright: Technically, gem art is de facto protected from the instant of creation. In practice, it is difficult to prove the priority of a design in the absence of a formally registered copyright.

Patents: A gem cut may not be novel enough to qualify for copyright protection but still be patentable, so long as it is different in some way from previous designs. The difficult part is deciding which kind of patent protection to apply for – utility or design. This is because in the case of jewellery, the distinction on which such decisions traditionally rest (that between an item's ornamental and functional qualities) no longer applies. Jewellery's function is to be ornamental! As a rule of thumb, if you've come up with a simple, geometrical gem cut that happens not to have been used before, you're better off applying for a design patent. If, on the other hand, you've devised a new cutting technique, go for the utility kind

Trade Dress: If a jeweller's designs are distinctive enough (in other words, if the public come to associate a particular style with a certain designer), they may qualify for protection as Trade Dress. The necessary recognition takes time to develop, but once established, Trade Dress protection can be extended indefinitely.

CELEBRITY INVENTORS

Zeppo Marx

Zeppo Marx, the youngest of the family, tended to play the 'straight man' in the brothers' films. He was also, in his time, the holder of two patents. The first was a coupling device for World War Two bombers. In 1945, it was used to release the atom bombs over Hiroshima and Nagasaki. Twenty-four years later, Zeppo patented an altogether nicer invention, a heart wristwatch monitor, together with Albert D Herman.

TEN MOST PIRATED AUTHORS
ON THE INTERNET, 2001

According to a survey carried out in by UK company
Envisional, the winners, or rather the losers, were:

1. Stephen King
2. JK Rowling
3. Terry Pratchett
4. Tom Clancy
5. Douglas Adams
6. JRR Tolkien
7. John Grisham
8. Iain M Banks
9. Irvine Welsh
10. Douglas Coupland

*In 2004, Envisional estimated the number of pirated
titles available on the net at 25–30,000.*

TRADEMARK OVERLOAD?

According to the United States Patent and Trademark Office, the
average Westerner on the average day encounters 1,500 trademarks. The
figure rises dramatically to up to 30,000 if he or she visits a supermarket.

JEAN TINGUELY

Most artists jealously protect the integrity of their work through copyright registration (where appropriate) and other intellectual property devices. The French will fight to the death to defend the individual's perpetual right not to have his or her creations interfered with. But the Swiss kinetic sculptor Jean Tinguely had a different approach. He liked to build machines that destroyed themselves. Tinguely's most celebrated (anti) creation was unveiled at the garden of New York's Museum of Modern Art in March 1960. 'Homage to New York' was an eight-metre high sculpture composed of, among other things, a bath tub, piano, radio, car horn and meteorological sounding balloon, several bottles and fire extinguishers, scraps of the American flag, playing cards, an oil canister, a hammer and saw, and about 80 bike, tricycle and pram wheels. It was powered by 15 engines. An audience of dinner-jacketed A-listers sat down to watch the machine destroy itself to its own accompaniment. Wheels whirred, piano keys tinkled and fireworks shot out in all directions. But something went wrong and the job had to be finished off by volunteers from the New York Fire Brigade.

'This is too awful to watch! Stop my good man, stop!
Felix thinks you're a hamster!'

QUOTE UNQUOTE

There is a patent office at the seat of government of
the universe, whose managers are as much interested
in the dispersion of seeds as anybody at Washington can be,
and their operations are infinitely more extensive and regular.
Henry David Thoreau, US poet, author and philosopher
The US Patent Office of the day had taken to distributing samples
of new varieties of seeds to the nation's farmers.

UNWILLING ANIMAL PIONEERS

The first parachutists were animals. Louis Lenormand, who invented
the parachute in 1783, had several of them test it from the roof of
Montpellier observatory. Joseph Montgolfier (the inventor of the
balloon) once dropped the same unfortunate sheep from the top of
the Papal Palace in Avignon six times in succession. And the first
parachute display in America, organised by Jean Pierre Blanchard in
1793, featured a dog, a cat and a squirrel floating down to Earth
together under the same canopy. Human beings stayed well clear
until 1797.

90 *Year in the twentieth century in which Tim Berners-Lee invented the http and*
    www internet protocols

ANOTHER JUMBLED INVENTOR

The name of which clean inventor is concealed in this anagram?
'I charm seed'
Answer on page 153.

THE BIKINI EMERGES FROM THE WAVES

The bikini was invented by two Frenchmen in 1946 and named after Bikini Atoll in the Marshall Islands, the site of recent atomic bomb tests. There had been similar garments before. Drawings of bikini-like costumes have been found on wall paintings dating from 1600 BC, conjuring up welcome visions of Raquel Welch in *One Million Years BC*. But Jacques Heim and Louis Reard revived the idea and popularised it. Heim had previously designed a micro-swimsuit called L'Atome' ('atom' in French) and advertised it as 'The world's smallest bathing suit'. After the designers had hit on the bikini, they hired a skywriter to introduce another slogan to the French Riviera: 'Bikini – smaller than the smallest bathing suit in the world.'

SIX THINGS YOU CANNOT
PATENT IN THE USA

- Laws of nature (eg e=mc^2),
- Physical phenomena (eg ice),
- Abstract ideas (philosophies, mathematical formulae),
- Literary, dramatic, musical, and artistic works (these can only be copyright protected),
- Inventions which are not useful,
- Inventions which are offensive to public morality (you couldn't, for instance, patent an item if it was only useful as a component of an atomic bomb).

CREATIVE COMPENSATION

The source of man's creativeness is in his deficiencies; he creates to compensate himself for what he lacks. He became *Homo faber* – a maker of weapons and tools – to compensate for his lack of specialised organs. He became *Homo ludens* – a player, tinker, and artist – to compensate for his lack of inborn skills. He became a speaking animal to compensate for his lack of the telepathic faculty by which animals communicate with each other. He became a thinker to compensate for the ineffectualness of his instincts.

A rather depressing account of the inventive impulse from the American author Eric Hoffer in
Reflections on the Human Condition

WHAT HATH GOD WROUGHT?
Text of the world's first electronic message, sent by Samuel Morse
from Washington DC to Baltimore in May 1844

WINNERS AND LOSERS IN PARODY CASES

Winners

In 1969, **Personality Posters Manufacturing Co** prevailed against the Girl Scouts of the USA in a trademark infringement case over a poster depicting a heavily pregnant Girl Scout above the legend 'Be Prepared'.

Lardashe Jeans. In 1987, Jordache Jeans filed suit for trade name infringement against Hogg Wyld Limited (later Oink Inc), a small New Mexican manufacturer of clothing for the larger lady. The two women owners had considered several self-deprecating names for their new line of jeans, including 'Vidal Sowsoon' and 'Calvin Swine', before settling on 'Lardashe'. The court ruled in their favour, stating that 'an intent to parody is not an intent to confuse the public'.

2 Live Crew. In 1994, the US Supreme Court upheld the rap band's right to parody the lyrics of Roy Orbison's *Oh Pretty Woman*, as it had recently done to hilarious effect in the single *Pretty Woman*.

Losers

The Chemical Corporation of America failed, in 1962, to persuade a court that its 'Where there's life... there's bugs' campaign for an insecticide-laced floor wax was a legitimate parody of Anheuser-Busch Inc's 'Where there's life... there's Bud' advertisements.

In 1987, the **Mutual of Omaha** insurance company successfully sued the manufacturers of a range of t-shirts and mugs featuring its 'Indian head' logo atop the slogan 'Mutant of Omaha'.

US PATENTS BY NUMBER

1	Traction wheels (1836)
10	Cutting dye wood (1836)
100	Patent withdrawn
1,000	Carriage spring for railroad cars (1838)
10,000	Paddle wheel (1863)
100,000	Horse sun-bonnet (1870)
1,000,000	Vehicle tyre (1911)

...the publishing rights to over 3,000 songs, including:
The Buddy Holly Catalogue
The songs from the musical *Grease*
The songs from the musical *Annie*

ACCIDENTAL INVENTIONS

Teflon

Teflon was invented in 1938 by a DuPont research chemist named Roy J Plunkett. One day he was experimenting with a coolant called TFE (tetrafluoroethylene) to establish its suitability for refrigeration purposes. For some reason, the pressurised cylinder of the gas filled earlier by Plunkett's assistant failed to discharge properly when the valve was opened. Throwing all safety rules out of the window, the pair decided to cut it open to see what had happened.

Instead of a violent explosion, they found that the gas had solidified inside the cylinder to form a strangely slippery white powder. Indeed, tests revealed that it was the slipperiest substance in existence. It was also inert and had an extremely high melting point.

DuPont registered Teflon as a trademark in 1945 and started marketing products coated with the miracle lubricant the following year. Since then, Teflon has not only been used for millions of frying pans, but also in microchips, rocket shields and spacesuits. The product was immortalised as the nickname of the supposedly unprosecutable New York gangster John 'Teflon' Gotti (nothing would stick) and has even been applied to the creaking joints of the Statue of Liberty.

IDEAS IN THE AIR

Literature is full of coincidences, which some love to believe are plagiarisms. There are thoughts always abroad in the air which it takes more wit to avoid than to hit upon.

Oliver Wendell Holmes

IP PARADOXES

Here's something to ponder. Did the person who invented the copyright symbol, or more importantly who first gave concrete expression to the idea in the form of a 'c' with a circle around it, automatically obtain intellectual property rights concerning its subsequent use (at least in theory)?

SILENCE IS GOLDEN

Music producer Mike Batt is best known to British audiences as the composer of the theme tune to *The Wombles*, a 1970s children's show about a clan of litter-obsessed furry creatures living on Wimbledon Common. More recently, he found himself enmeshed in a curious legal battle after the release of The Planets' album *Classical Graffiti*. Batt had inserted 60 seconds of silence to separate the 12 main tracks from four supplementary remixes, naming it *A One Minute Silence* in honour of John Cage's seminal noiseless symphony *4'33'* (1952).

Two months after *Classical Graffiti*'s chart debut, Mr Batt received a letter from the Mechanical-Copyright Protection Society (MCPS). 'It informed me' as the producer dryly put it 'that my silence was a copyright infringement on Cage's silence'. The letter added that an initial payment of around four hundred pounds had been made to the administrators of the Cage catalogue.

In the end, the opposing parties agreed to stage a concert, thereby allowing the public to assess the respective merits of the compositions. Batt went first, leading The Planets through a spirited rendition of *A One Minute's Silence*. Then a Mr Riddle, representing the Cage camp, introduced a young clarinettist, who proceeded (not) to play *4'33'*. The occasion, however, failed to dampen Mike Batt's sense of grievance. He has subsequently registered silent compositions varying in duration from one second to 10 minutes, and is particularly jealous of the rights adhering to *4'32'* and *4'34'*. 'If there's ever a Cage performance where they come in a second shorter or longer,' he has warned, 'then it's mine.'

MONTY PYTHON PLEASE TAKE NOTE

Jonathan Swift wrote under many pseudonyms, including T Tinker, Andrew Tripe, Isaac Bickerstaff, Martinus Scribberus and Simon Wagstaff. But the greatest has to be SPAM.

WELL DEFINED

Eagle

Not, according to a suit filed in 1998, a large carnivorous bird, but a member of a 1970s rock band best known for the song *Hotel California*. The Eagles claimed, a touch absurdly, that the National Foundation to Protect America's Eagles (NFPAE) had infringed their copyright by registering the internet address 'eagles.org' and the phone number 1-800-2-Eagles.

The band dropped the case in 2001.

FOOTBALLERS AND INTELLECTUAL PROPERTY

In 2000, the World Intellectual Property Organisation (WIPO) ordered Sallen Enterprises, the operators of a website devoted to St Paul's correspondence with the residents of Corinth, to hand over the domain name corinthians.com to a Brazilian soccer club. The fact that the Pauline epistles predated the Sao Paulo team (founded in 1910) by some 1865 years cut little ice with WIPO. A one-man panel found that 'the posting was fabricated to divert consumers, or more generally the public interested in visiting what they think is the site of the well known Brazilian soccer team.' Naturally the decision went down like a lead balloon in Christian circles.

THE BIRTH OF THE RUBIK'S CUBE

It was wonderful, to see how, after only a few turns, the colours became mixed, apparently in random fashion. It was tremendously satisfying to watch this colour parade. Like after a nice walk when you have seen many lovely sights you decide to go home, after a while I decided it was time to go home, let us put the cubes back in order. And it was at that moment that I came face to face with the Big Challenge: What is the way home? ... [I was] staring at a piece of writing written in a secret code. But for me, it was a code I myself had invented! Yet I could not read it. This was such an extraordinary situation that I simply could not accept it.

**Erno Rubik, from an unpublished manuscript
called *Rubik on Rubik***

LIGHTEN UP GEORGE

In July 2001, George Lucas, fiercely protective of his movies, filed a trademark infringement suit against medical-instruments makers Minrad, Inc. for calling a line of laser-guided surgical scalpels 'Light Sabers'. Lucas had come up with the phrase, which described a luminous weapon wielded by the sinister Darth Vader and the Jedi Knights, prior to the release of the first *Star Wars* film in 1977. 'Any deficiencies or faults in the quality of the defendant's goods,' his lawyers declared, 'are likely to reflect negatively upon, tarnish and seriously injure the reputation which Lucasfilm has established for goods and services marketed under its Light Saber mark.' Minrad countered that they couldn't honestly see their product reducing revenues from the sale of 'toy swords'. The suit appears not to have been followed up; presumably the dispute was settled out of court.

10 BIGGEST AWARDS IN IP CASES

The companies mentioned first were either victorious in an intellectual property infringement lawsuit, or negotiated a deal in the absence/presence of one. 'P' stands for patents, 'C' for copyrights

Amount	Year	Parties	Action
$2.5bn	2002	Major League Baseball v Fox Television	C License
$1.725bn	1996	NCAA Basketball v CBS	C License
$1bn	2000	SnapTrack v Eastman Kodak	Buyout
$873m	1991	Polaroid v Eastman Kodak	P Lawsuit
$820m	2001	Hallmark Entertainment v Crown Media	C Buyout
$700m	1997	Digital v Intel	P Lawsuit
$505m	2002	Igen International v Roche Holding	P Lawsuit
$500m+	1990	Texas Instruments v Toshiba	P Settlement
$500m	2002	Paramount Pictures v Kirch Media	C License
$500m	2002	City of Hope Nat Med Cent. v Genentech	P Lawsuit
$500m	1998	College Football v ABC	C License

Source: www.patenting-art.com/economic/awards.htm

THE WIT AND WISDOM OF WINNIE

Winston Churchill was always ready with a *bon mot*, particularly when dining with the great and the good at Chartwell, his house in Kent. On one occasion he found himself sitting next to Charlie Chaplin, and asked the comic legend what his next role was to be. 'Jesus Christ!' said Chaplin, who had barely finished his previous movie. 'Ah, but have you cleared the rights?' growled Winnie.

A BITE FROM THE APPLE?

Beatles fan Steve Jobs could lose a large chunk of his Apple to his idols. The Fab Four's company, Apple Corps, is involved in a legal battle with Jobs' Apple Computer, claiming the hardware manufacturer is in breach of a 1991 agreement forbidding it from using the trademark for any application 'whose principle content is music'. The two companies have been involved in a number of court battles over the years involving the use of the Apple trademark. Gossip suggests that an out of court settlement could be imminent of a magnitude to dwarf the US$26.5 million Computer paid Corps as part of the 1991 agreement.

CHINESE SENSIBILITIES

The people of China are growing accustomed to Western multinationals plundering their heritage for marketing purposes. American Express has been donating money to the Forbidden City since 1987, and its name is now displayed on signs throughout the complex. Starbucks opened a branch inside the Forbidden City in late 2000, and Richemont, the European luxury goods conglomerate, recently staged an exhibition of 600 Swiss watches in the former Imperial Palace. The Great Wall is used to advertise everything from paint to toothpaste. 'These big glorious monuments can... reinforce an image of stability and reliability,' comments Tom Doctoroff, area director at J Walter Thompson in Shanghai. But as Toyota discovered in 2003, such cultural appropriation needs be handled delicately. A company

advert depicting a traditional Chinese stone lion paying homage to a Toyota sports utility vehicle, with the slogan 'you have to respect it', caused outrage among veterans of the Sino-Japanese war. Apparently similar lions had stood along the Marco Polo Bridge in Beijing, the site of the 1937 clash between Japanese and Chinese troops that triggered the conflict.

Chinese advertising laws are notoriously vague, but the key to mounting a successful campaign is obtaining the blessing of the Chinese Advertising Association (CAA), the governmental body responsible for vetting commercials. CAA's President, Yang Peiqing, has defined the organisation's philosophy thus: 'The release of an advertisement should not only produce a better economic result but a better result in spiritual civilisation.'

CELEBRITY INVENTORS

Hedy Lamarr

Hedy Lamarr (born Hedwig Kiesler on November 9, 1913), the Austrian-born actress fondly remembered for her role in Mel Brooks' *Blazing Saddles*, also happened to co-invent the radio-controlled torpedo. She had first mooted the idea before her move to America in 1937, while married to the arms dealer Fritz Mandl, but abandoned it when she found out how easily radio signals could be jammed. She revisited it in 1939, while talking to the composer George Antheil. They realised that if the frequency of radio signals could be changed at random intervals (a process known as 'frequency hopping'), they would be just the job for guiding torpedoes. In 1941, the pair filed a patent for their invention, but it lapsed in 1959, unused.

Hedy, who died in 2000, lived to see her invention adopted by the satellite communications industry, though too late to earn her any money. Now known as 'spread spectrum', it is to make mobile/cell phone calls more secure against eavesdropping.

PROTECTING THE NATURAL WORLD
(IN AN INTELLECTUAL PROPERTY SENSE...)

Determining whether a design based on a 'literal' interpretation of nature is amenable to intellectual property protection can be a tricky business. In 1999, for instance, Vickery Design, a New Mexico candle manufacturer, tried to prevent a rival company from making alternative versions of its speciality: a candle in the shape of a corn cob. The Court ruled against Vickery, essentially because its design was just too good. Its candles reflected the way corn occurred in nature so accurately that they were deemed uncopyrightable.

In 1993, however, a court decided that Wildlife Express was entitled to prevent Carol Wright Sales from selling duffel bags similar to its own, which featured faithful representations of the heads and tails of various animals. This time, the judge ruled that the designs were copyrightable because they were imaginative artistic expressions. The heads and tails couldn't be lifelike representations because they were separated by duffel bags.

Artistic users of the natural world may have better luck registering a design patent. In one of the earliest reported cases, Wood v. Dolby (1881), a jeweller was awarded monetary damages when a competitor copied his patented design featuring a bird, a twig and diamonds

QUOTE UNQUOTE

It is a strange fact that important inventions are often made almost simultaneously by different persons in different parts of the world.
Alexander Graham Bell, Scottish inventor

LANDMARKS IN THE HISTORY
OF GENETIC PATENTS

In 1980, the US Supreme Court ruled for the first time that a non-plant organism could be patented. The Diamond v. Chakrabarty case revolved around a bacterium genetically engineered to break down oil spills. In a close decision, the judges decided that the creature met the necessary criteria for patenting, being a 'manufacture' and a 'composition of matter'. The Court did, however, make a point of declaring itself 'without competence' to judge the merits of arguments warning of apocalyptic consequences if life was deemed patentable.

By 2003, the United States Patent and Trademark Office had granted more than 400 patents for higher life-forms.

US plant patent number for a freesia with large light lavender-violet flowers (1934)

Prior to the unveiling of the Segway, journalists had noticed the impressive list of investors in the secret project and caught whiff of a big story. They had named the mystery invention 'Ginger'.

Segway LLC, the business founded by inventor and entrepreneur Dean Kamen to transform the way people work and live, today announced the much-anticipated debut of the Segway Human Transporter (HT), the first self-balancing, electric-powered transportation machine. With dimensions no larger than the average adult body and the ability to emulate human balance, the Segway HT uses the same space as a pedestrian, and can go wherever a person can walk. The Segway HT will allow people to go farther, move more quickly, and increase the amount they can carry anywhere they currently walk.

'The Segway HT is an enhancement to personal mobility that will allow people to make better use of their time,' said Dean Kamen, Segway's chairman & CEO and the man with the technological vision behind the human transporter. 'Ultimately, the Segway HT can make urban environments more livable by providing a solution to short-distance travel. If the Segway HT is widely adopted, it could help solve major urban problems, such as pollution, congestion and livability.'

The company will produce three distinct models: the i-series optimizes range and speed across a variety of terrain; the e-series is designed for business applications where it is necessary to carry cargo – up to 75 pounds in addition to the rider; the p-series will be ideal for densely populated areas, both indoors and out. The Segway HT's footprint is narrower than the average adult's shoulders and its length is no greater than a large shoe. And it's quiet – designed to emit only a barely audible harmonic hum.

Segway HT will first be introduced for commercial use. Initial applications include large scale manufacturing plants and warehousing operations, travel and tourism, public safety, corporate and campus transportation, mail, package and product delivery.
Segway LLC Press Release, 2001

THE WORLD'S FIRST COMPUTER PROGRAMMER...

...was a mathematician named Ada Byron. She published her first programmes in 1843, for use with the mechanical digital computer recently developed by Charles Babbage. Her system was based on punch-cards.

SOME US PATENT 'FIRSTS'

1790 Samuel Hopkins of Pittsford, Vermont becomes the first person to be issued a federal patent in the United States. The invention in question was a method for the 'making of Pot Ash by a new apparatus & process'.

1809 Mary Dixon Kies is the first woman to be granted a patent by the US Patent Office. She had devised a new technique of weaving straw with silk and thread.

1821 Thomas L Jennings is the first African-American man to be granted a patent, for the invention of dry cleaning. It is some-times erroneously assumed that the first African American patent holder was the Henry Blair of Glenross, Maryland, who patented a corn planter in 1834. The confusion arises because, in the only instance of racial speci-fication in the early records, the patent documentation refers to Blair as 'a colored man'.

1836 The majority of the 10,000-odd patents issued by the US Patent office during the first 46 years of its existence are destroyed in a fire. About 2,800 are eventually salvaged, and given a number ending in an 'x'. They are now known as X-Patents.

SCRAMBLED LYRICS

The songwriter who penned the following tribute to the humble egg was so struck by the catchiness of the tune he had composed for it that he was sure he must have plagiarised it from somebody else's work. Given the all clear by music industry execs, the song was released with a rather more soulful set of lyrics and has since been covered over 3,000 times. What was it? (We've just provided the first verse – there was more).

> *Scrambled Eggs,*
> *Have an omelette with some Muenster cheese,*
> *Put your dishes in the wash-bin please,*
> *So I can clean the scrambled eggs.*

Answer on page 153.

STAR WARS

When Ronald Reagan started to refer to the Pentagon's Strategic Defence System (a scheme to equip satellites with missiles to take out any warheads that might be fired from the Soviet block) as 'Star Wars', the film director George Lucas filed suit against the administration for nicking his phrase. He lost.

OBSCURE PATENTS

*Uncle Septimus took night diving to a whole
new level when he invented the Aquavelocipede.*

SARA LEE OWNS...

Although best known for its frozen desserts and cheesecakes, the Sara
Lee Corporation owns a bewildering variety of brands, including:

Wonderbra (women's underwear)
Playtex (ditto)
Kiwi (shoe polish)
Douwe Egberts (coffee)
Ball Park (franks, corn dogs and smoked sausages)
Champion (athletic apparel)
Ambi Pur (air fresheners)
Sanex (bath and toiletry products)

MOTION MARKS

A few registered trademarks consist of not one, but a series of images,
such as a clip of film or a computer animation. The Netscape 'aster-
oid shower' is one example, as is the sequence at the beginning of
Tristar movies where a winged horse charges towards the audience
and then soars into flight.

Everyone is a genius at least once a year; a real genius has his original ideas closer together.
GC Lichtenberg, German writer and physicist

AND YOU THOUGHT YOU WERE HAVING PROBLEMS?

...The first step to be took, in Patenting the invention, was to prepare a petition unto Queen Victoria... A declaration before a Master in Chancery was to be added to it. That, we likewise drew up. After a deal of trouble I found out a Master, in Southampton Buildings, Chancery Lane, nigh Temple Bar, where I made the declaration, and paid eighteen-pence. I was told to take the declaration and petition to the Home Office, in Whitehall, where I left it to be signed by the Home Secretary (after I had found the office out), and where I paid two pound, two, and sixpence. In six days he signed it, and I was told to take it to the Attorney-General's chambers, and leave it there for a report. I did so, and paid four pound, four... The Attorney-General made what they called a Report-of-course (my invention being, as William Butcher had delivered before starting, unopposed), and I was sent back with it to the Home Office. They made a Copy of it, which was called a Warrant. For this warrant, I paid seven pound, thirteen, and six. It was sent to the Queen, to sign. The Queen sent it back, signed. The

Home Secretary signed it again. The gentleman throwed it at me when I called, and said, 'Now take it to the Patent Office in Lincoln's Inn'... I found myself losing heart.

At the Patent Office in Lincoln's Inn, they made 'a draft of the Queen's bill,' of my invention, and a 'docket of the bill.' I paid five pound, ten, and six, for this. They 'engrossed two copies of the bill; one for the Signet Office, and one for the Privy-Seal Office.' I paid one pound, seven, and six, for this. Stamp duty over and above, three pound. The Engrossing Clerk of the same office engrossed the Queen's bill for signature. I paid him one pound, one. Stamp-duty, again, one pound, ten. I was next to take the Queen's bill to the Attorney-General again, and get it signed again. I took it, and paid five pound more. I fetched it away, and took it to the Home Secretary again. He sent it to the Queen again. She signed it again. I paid seven pound, thirteen, and six, more, for this... I was quite wore out, patience and pocket.

But I hadn't nigh done yet...

Charles Dickens,
A Poor Man's Tale of a Patent

NEW BRAND NAME NAMES

In 2003, an interesting trend in infant nomenclature was revealed by psychology professor Cleveland Evans of Bellevue University, Nebraska. It seems that Americans are increasingly naming their children after their favourite brands.

Dr Cleveland's study of social security records for the year 2000 turned up the following titbits:

- There were two little boys, one in Michigan and one in Texas, called ESPN after the sports channel.
- Car brands were a popular source of names. Twenty-two girls were registered as Infiniti and five were called Celica.
- Seven boys were called Del Monte. There were 49 male Canons, after the camera firm, and six lads named Courvoisier. There were also six Timberlands and seven Denims.

HIJACKED LOGOS AND ECSTASY

Ecstasy tablets illicitly adorned with the trademarks of all the following companies have been seized by British authorities:

Motorola • Calvin Klein

Armani • Disney

Playboy • Opel • Rolex

Most notorious, however, were the millions of pills 'branded' with the three-diamond logo of the Mitsubishi Corporation that flooded the UK club scene during the mid 1990s, known for its high MDMA content, it was nicknamed the 'Mitsi'.

NAPPY CHIC

In 1977, a court ruled that the 'original' Gucci had every right to be concerned about the appearance on the market of unlicensed 'Gucci Goo' diaper bags. After all, the connotations scarcely enhanced the company's glamourous image. But times have moved on, and in distancing themselves from the attempt to provide a chic solution to a perennial maternal dilemma, Gucci may have missed a trick. In the autumn of 2002, Louis Vuitton came out with its first-ever baby product: a monogrammed diaper bag featuring a built-in bottle holder, a cotton baby blanket, a zip pocket for wipes and a washable hypoallergenic changing mat. There were also plenty of compartments for mum's accoutrements. The bag retailed for a cool US$1,020.

Thomas Alva Edison

During his lifetime, the 'Wizard of Menlo Park' was awarded 1093 US patents. He applied for the first, an electric vote recorder, at the age of 21. The world would have been unimaginably different without Edison, who invented both the phonograph and the motion picture. It would also have been a lot darker. Edison did not actually invent the electric light-bulb, but he did make it economically viable. Mind you, he did back the occasional loser, as when he championed the merits of DC rather than AC power.

1868 Edison's applies for his first patent, for an an electronic vote recorder

1874 Edison invents the quadruplex telegraph.

1875 Edison devises an 'autographic press' kit, to be used by businesses to make copies of documents. The kit includes an electric pen, a small battery, a press, ink and supplies.

1877 Edison produces a telephone transmitter that allows voices to be transmitted at a higher volume and with greater clarity than Alexander Graham Bell's version.

1879 Using a small carbonised filament, and an improved vacuum inside the bulb, Edison produces a reliable, long-lasting source of light.

1880 The commercial production of electric lamps begins at the Edison Lamp Works in Menlo Park.

1881 Edison executes 23 patent applications on electric lighting.

1882 During the spring and summer Edison executes 53 patent applications covering electric lighting, electric railways, and secondary batteries. He executes an additional 34 patent applications covering electric lighting and electric railways in autumn that same year. 1882 becomes the most prolific year of his inventing career.

1885 Edison begins the process of patenting the kinetoscope and kinetograph.

1888 Edison makes 22 patent applications for phonographs and cylinder records.

1896 Edison introduces the Edison Home Phonograph, a cheap, spring-motor driven record player.

1900 Edison applies for a patent for a method of mass producing cylinder phonograph records.

1902 The 'Wizard of Menlo Park' initiates production of alkaline storage batteries.

5 TRADEMARKED SMELLS

- *A high impact, fresh, floral fragrance reminiscent of plumeria blossoms* for use with yarn and thread. Now lapsed. (US)
- *A scent mark having the scent of bubble gum* for use with oil-based metal cutting fluid and oil based metal removing fluid for industrial metal working. (US)
- *The scent of bitter* (beer) applied to darts flights. (UK)
- *The fragrance of rose petals*, applied to tyres (to make them smell nice in the event of skids). (UK)
- *The scent of freshly mown grass* applied to tennis balls. (EC)

The US Trademark Trial and Appeal Board has held that a 'fragrance can be capable of serving as a trademark to identify and distinguish' goods, but only when it is not an 'inherent attribute' of the product. This rules out perfumes, scented household products and so on. The UK and the EU allocate their trademarks in a similar fashion.

NOW THAT'S ENTERTAINMENT!

MBN, a South Korean cable television channel, screened an unmissable series in 2001 entitled *HH Nahm's Funny and Interesting Intellectual Property Anecdotes*. Clips of the eponymous presenter in action can be downloaded from his company's website (www.nahm-patent.co.kr). Laugh along as he regales you with the saga of the Chef who Stole the Secret Recipe of Ih-dong galbi (barbecued ribs). Weep at tales of the trademark vicissitudes afflicting manufacturers of saewoo-kkang (shrimp confectionery). Or try to; unfortunately, it's all in Korean.

'WANTON' PLAGIARISM

Beatles' fans might find that the following lines of poetry ring a bell:

> *Golden slumbers kiss your eyes,*
> *Smiles awake you when you rise.*
> *Sleep, pretty wantons, do not cry,*
> *And I will sing a lullaby.*

They are, of course, the lyrics of *Golden Slumber* from the album *Abbey Road*. Or near enough: substitute the word 'darling' for 'wantons' and you're there.' But the words were actually penned by English poet Thomas Dekker. Although the copyright had obviously lapsed several centuries beforehand, some Fab Four fans were a mite disillusioned when this piece of 'creative borrowing' came to light.

'I want to register these as my trademark.'

COPYRIGHTING MOTHER TERESA

When Mother Teresa died in 1997 (in the same week as the Zairian Dictator Mobutu and Princess Diana), it was revealed that she had stipulated in her will that no one should use her name for commercial transactions. In 2003, her religious order, the Missionaries of Charity, announced it was taking legal action to ensure that the wishes of the Albanian-born nun were respected. Her successor, Sister Nirmala, told reporters that 'We are seeking legal protection for the use of our logo, and also want such protection for the name of Mother Teresa and that of the Missionaries of Charity'.

Sister Nirmala had been dismayed to see a rash of schools and hospitals in Southern India adopting the names after her death. She had been still more dismayed to learn that a bank in Hyderabad had tried to open as the Mother Teresa Co-operative.

In Lake Jackson, Texas, the proprietor of a local delicatessen remained unrepentant. 'My name is Teresa, my grandmother's name is Teresa,' said Teresa Polimeno, the Italian-born owner of Mother Teresa's Fine Foods. 'Nobody in their right mind is going to pretend to be Mother Teresa.'

PRODUCTS WITH DISMAL
FIRST YEAR US SALES

VW Beetle – 300 cars
(Sales peaked at over 200,000 in 1962. On 30 July 2003, the 21,529,464th and final original Beetle rolled off the production line in Puebla, Mexico).

Scrabble – 532 sets
(Annual US sales now vary from one to two million).

Liquid Paper – 1,200 bottles
(Liquid Paper was invented in 1951 by Bette Nesmith, mother of Michael Nesmith of Monkees fame. By the time she sold her company to Gillette in 1979, the product was generating US$38 million in annual sales).

Remington Typewriter – eight units (This was the first 'commercial' typewriter, introduced in 1874. By 1910, two million typewriters were being sold annually in the USA. By the late 1980s, global sales had reached 10 million units per annum).

Coca-Cola – 25 bottles
(In 2002, Coca Cola sold 5.6 billion cases of soft drinks in the USA, equivalent to 134.4 billion 8oz cans).

IDENTIFY THE GENERIC NAMES

Which of the following names are generic and which are enforceable trademarks? Clue: there are five of the former.

Kleenex • Marmite • Escalator
Biro • Dictaphone • Vaseline
Coke • Xerox • Ping-Pong
Valium • Quarter Pounder • Sellotape
Gramophone • Thermos • Tupperware
Formica • Pyrex • Lurex
Brylcreem • Cellophane • Frisbee
Shredded Wheat • Stetson • Linoleum

Answer on page 153.

THE ART OF GOLF

In a landmark case, the golfer Tiger Woods took Alabama-based artist Rick Rush to court for painting a picture of him in action at the Master's tournament in Augusta in 1997. Eldrick Tiger Woods Corporation alleged copyright violation, arguing that it had exclusive rights to the Tiger's name, likeness and signature.

In 2000, a district judge ruled in Rush's favour, and street cartoonists everywhere breathed a sigh of relief. The decision was later upheld by the US Court of Appeals.

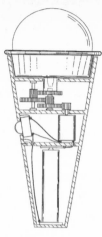

For those times when it's just too much effort to turn your hand round. US Design Patent No. 5,971,829

WELL DEFINED

g

Not, apparently, the lowercase form of the seventh letter of the alphabet, but a trademark belonging to the hip-hop performer Warren g. In 1997, lawyers representing the said rap artist sued country star Garth (or garth) Brooks for the unauthorised use of their client's little 'g'.

Brooks then countersued, claiming that the rap star had stolen the idea from him. The musicians settled out of court in March 1998, with each agreeing to allow the other to continue using his particular version of the troublesome letter (g's accompanied by the words 'funk music'; Brooks' enclosed within a circle).

Brooks later explained the reason for his change of heart 'I learned from Warren g and Wron g (the star's manager) that the letter "g" has a special significance to them and to some members of their community in that it symbolises kids and young people who have risen above drugs and violence and who are worthy of respect because of their positive contributions to the world... Now knowing how much the symbol "g" means to Warren, I will strive to reach the standard that the "g" represents to him and to his community.'

LEXUS

Hip-hop has done a lot for US car manufacturer Lexus, with several rap artists eulogising its products. Recently, however, the association took a sinister new turn when members of the fraternity discovered that the company's L-shaped logo looked remarkably like a pistol when rotated through 180 degrees. It is now a *de riguer* gangsta accessory. Oh well, at least it shows more ambition than the 1980s Volkswagen phase.

THOUGHT LEADERS:
PATENTS THAT HAVE CHANGED THE WORLD.

Z-Y position indicator for a display system
(otherwise known as a mouse).

At age 25, Doug Engelbart resolved to 'do something to improve human capacity to deal with the increasing complexity of the world.' In 1968, after 20 years of work, he began to realise this dream, demonstrating a graphic computer system, controlled by an attached keyboard and accompanied by a small chunky box, attached by tail-like cord – affectionately known as a 'mouse'. This was a key element of the NLS (oN Line System), which he and colleagues at the Stanford research institute hoped would usher in a revolution of what we now know as distributed collaborative learning.

THAT'S ALL RIGHT, ELVIS

From the first of January 2005, anyone will be able to bring out a song that has been on release in Europe for over 50 years without alerting the copyright owner of the original recording. This means that, unlike the US, where songs are protected for 95 years, the owners of recordings more than 50 years old will no longer benefit from European royalties. Since 1955 was a seminal year for rock and roll, we must brace ourselves for a torrent of boy- and girl-band covers. Among the first songs to be affected are Elvis Presley's *That's All Right* and Bill Haley and the Comets' *Shake Rattle and Roll*.

Beatles' songs, which form one of the most lucrative catalogues in history, are the next great targets on the horizon. They start to come out of copyright on the first of January 2013. However, before you go out and record your own version of *Love Me Do*, bear in mind that while the recording will no longer be protected, the song still will be for another 20 years. Writers and composers will still be entitled to royalties, even when performers and record companies no longer are. So European covers won't be free – they'll just be cheaper.

THE 'GAME' OF INTELLECTUAL PROPERTY

Man was born to be rich, or, inevitably grows rich by the use of his faculties; by the union of thought with nature. Property is an intellectual production. The game requires coolness, right reasoning, promptness, and patience in the players. Cultivated labor drives out brute labor. An infinite number of shrewd men, in infinite years, have arrived at certain best and shortest ways of doing, and this accumulated skill in arts, cultures, harvestings, curings, manufactures, navigations, exchanges, constitutes the worth of our world to-day.

Ralph Waldo Emerson, *The Conduct of Life*

QUOTE UNQUOTE

If the pig had been exactly the same as the pig that I designed, I could have stopped them from using it.
Pink Floyd songwriter Roger Waters.
After he left the band in the mid-1980s, Waters had agreed to allow the remaining members to retain the name 'Pink Floyd', but been less accommodating about the giant pink pig balloons traditionally flown at Floyd gigs. Guitarist David Gilmour had circumvented the problem by designing a new pig featuring a less than polite body part.

PATENT MODELS

In the early days of the US patent system, all applicants were required to submit a small-scale model of their inventions to demonstrate how they worked. The maximum dimensions were 12" by 12". This was fine if you were a nimble-fingered thimble designer, but rather more onerous if you were a clumsy dam builder.

Congress abolished the legal requirement for Patent models in 1870, but the Patent Office continued to demand them until 1880. Some inventors were still submitting models at the close of the century, but this was entirely voluntary.

There is a thriving market for these dinky historical items among collectors – have a look on eBay. Many patent models are remarkable feats of engineering, particularly miniaturised versions of complex industrial and domestic machinery. There is a special charm in a tiny working washing machine or a Lilliputian water-turbine. Some patent models go for thousands of dollars.

FAIR USE, BUT NOT IN THE MOVIES

As many film-makers have discovered to their cost, US Trademark and Right of Publicity law make no formal provision for 'fair use' (Copyright law is a different matter entirely). This is a blessing in terms of combating the practice of product placement, but the law has caused the use of real world objects in movies to become fraught with difficulty. Here are a few of the casualties, as noted by the author Lawrence Lessig:

Batman Forever – In one scene, the Batmobile was shown driving through a courtyard. Its architect claimed copyright violation and demanded compensation His suit was rejected, but the release of the film was delayed.

Twelve Monkeys – The film was stopped by a court 28 days after its release when a furniture designer claimed that a chair featured in the film illegally resembled one of his own.

The Devil's Advocate – The release was delayed by two days after a sculptor complained about one of his pieces appearing in a background shot without his consent.

USELESS PATENTS

'Wearable Seating Apparatus'

There's not always a free seat available, but why worry when you could come prepared! Suspiciously resembling a cushion strapped to your behind when not fully deployed, GB patent no. 2,267,208 is a portable seating apparatus worn around the waist so that you are always ready to take a seat – even if there are none in sight.

THE FACTS OF THE FAX

When would you imagine the world's first fax was sent? The 1970s? The 1960s? The 1950s at a pinch?

The answer turns out to be 1907*. In that year, Arthur Korn transmitted a photograph from Munich to Berlin using a wire technology he had begun working on five years earlier.

* *A primitive version of the fax had been patented by Scottish inventor Alexander Bain as early as 1843, but Korn's device allowed the first inter-city transmissions.*

'Why, this is the best idea since... since... er...'

'WELL KNOWN'

What, exactly, makes a trademark 'well known'? Ironically, the concept is not clearly defined, but the following criteria have been suggested*:

1. The degree of recognition
2. Whether the mark has a reputation, is registered and enforced geographically
3. The extent and duration of usage and of advertising and publicity accorded
4. The degree of exclusivity and the nature and extent of use of the same or similar mark by third parties
5. The degree of inherent or acquired distinctiveness
6. The nature of the goods or services and the channels of trade for them
7. The degree to which the reputation of the mark symbolises quality goods
8. The extent of the commercial value attributed to the mark.

* *European Trade Mark Harmonization Regulation, Council Reg (EC) No. 40/94 of 20.12.93 on the Community Trade Mark.*

Richard Branson has taken brand extension to the limit with his Virgin group of companies. It all began with a small record label and the propitious decision to sign the Sex Pistols, but the bearded wonder's empire now encompasses 41 sub-brands in the UK alone according to the company website:

Virgin Active *(health clubs)*
Virgin Atlantic *(the airline)*
Virgin Atlantic Cargo
Virgin Balloon Flights
Virgin Bikes
Virgin Books
Virgin Brides
Virgin Business Solutions
Virgin Cars
Virgin Cosmetics
Virgin Credit Card
Virgin D3 *(develops online student campaigns)*
Virgin Drinks
Virgin Experience Days
Virgin Express
Virgin Galactic *(book your space flight years in advance)*
Virgin Games *(an online casino etc)*
Virgin Holidays
Virgin Home *(gas, electricity etc)*
Virgin Incentives *(staff motivation techniques)*
Virgin Limobike
Virgin Megastores UK
Virgin Mobile *(cellphones)*
Virgin Money *(loans, insurance, credit cards)*
Virgin Radio
Virgin Trains
Virgin Unite *(a charitable arm)*
Virgin Ware UK *(women's underwear)*
Virgin Wines
Virgin.com *(company portal)*
Virgin Net *(an ISP service)*
VirginStudent.com *(a website for students)*
Babylon *(a London restaurant)*
Kasbah Tamadot *(a resort in Morocco's Atlas mountains)*
Limited Edition *(a chain of exclusive hotels)*
Necker Island *(Branson's getaway in the British Virgin Islands)*
The Roof Gardens *(a bar/restaurant/venue in Kensington)*
Man was born to be rich *(online rail-booking service)*
Ulusaba *(RB's private game reserve in South Africa)*
V Festival *(a summer music fest)*
V2 Music *(the UK's biggest independent record label)*

CELEBRITY INVENTORS

Gary Burghoff

Best known for playing Radar O'Reilly in the television series M*A*S*H, the actor Gary Burghoff is clearly something of a fisherman. Or so the patents awarded to him would suggest. These include a 'Fish attractor device', an 'Enhanced fish attractor device', a fishing rod, and, somewhat incongruously, a 'Toilet seat lifting handle'.

WHO YOU GONNA CALL? – 'MY LAWYER!'

When Huey Lewis first heard Ray Parker Jr's No.1 hit *Ghostbusters* in 1984 (from the movie of the same name), it struck him that the song sounded uncannily like his hit *I Want a New Drug* from the previous year. Lewis sued Parker for copyright infringement and settled in 1995 for an undisclosed sum. Unfortunately, despite agreeing not to discuss the case in public, he proceeded to insult Parker on VH1. Result: another lawsuit.

THE PERILS OF FAKES

Counterfeit goods containing all sorts of nasties have been seized in the UK in recent years. Here are some salutary examples:

1. Booze – Bottles of Scotch, Vodka and alcopops containing methylated spirits and/or antifreeze. These substances can cause blindness.

2. Fake Tellytubby clothing – potentially lethal as highly flammable.

3. Fake Tetley tea bags – containing metal filings, floor sweepings and rodent droppings.

4. Washing powder – containing caustic soda. This burns the skin on contact.

5. Fake perfume – often turns out to incorporate urine as a chemical stabiliser.

PRINCESS DI P

One of the first entrepreneurs out of the traps in the race to cash in on the death of Princess Diana was Andre Engelhardt of Grosskarolinenfeld in Bavaria. Within hours of her fatal car crash in August 1997, Mr Engelhardt was in Munich registering the name 'Lady Di' as a trademark for a range of lingerie and perfume.

While Engelhardt admitted that he had no first-hand knowledge of the Princess's taste in undies, he explained the thinking behind his 'Lady Di' lingerie line shortly before its launch in 1999. 'Diana was a young, energetic and very beautiful woman,' he told Reuters TV, 'and I really doubt that she wore some old-fashioned underwear underneath her fancy dresses.'

Although Buckingham Palace was not best pleased, it was left to the Princess Diana Memorial Fund to contest Engelhardt's application. But the fund was unsuccessful and Engelhardt went on to rake in a tidy sum by licensing the name 'Lady Di' to perfume and underwear manufacturers.

TRADEMARKS ON CANVAS

The following works feature registered UK trademarks:

Artist	Work	Date	Trademark(s)	UK TM
George Adomeit (1879–1967)	A Cool Refreshing Drink	1931	Coca-Cola	427817
Richard Estes (1936–)	Canada Dry	1971	Canadian Club Coca-Cola Sony 7 UP	281512 427817 807375 716976
Edward Hopper (1882–1967)	Gas	1940	Winged Horse Mobilgas	641370 676079
Edouard Manet (1832–1883)	Bar at the Folies-Bergère	1882	Bass Triangle	1
Louise Jopling (1844–1933)	Home Bright, Hearts Light	1896	Sunlight Soap	280138
Sir John E Millais (1829–1896)	A Child's World	1886	Pears Soap	97230
Andy Warhol (1928–1987)	Five Coke Bottles	1962	Coca-Cola	2000546
	Can of Campbell's Soup	1964	Campbell's	672290

WEIRD DOMAIN NAMES

1. gross.com (a legal firm based in Fairfax, Virginia)
2. sasquatch.com
3. skank.com (Swedish urban clothing manufacturer)
4. boogers.com
5. stubby.org (website of the Stubblesfield family)
   (With thanks to: www.bspot.com)

A STRANGE URBAN MYTH

Somehow the idea has gained currency that the 'spot' on a can of 7UP is a form of homage to its inventor who was an albino. In fact, Charles Leiper Grigg was not an albino and the spot only appears to have been introduced during the 1970s.

In 1987, Cadbury Schweppes introduced a cartoon character based on the red dot motif on its trademarked cans. 'Spot' appeared in 7UP advertisements until 1995.

Number of international PCT patent applications originating in Hungary 115
in 2003

BRANDS ON THE BRAIN

In 2002, *The New Scientist* reported the findings of a study carried out at UCLA into how the human brain deals with brand names. 'It is surprising', said Eran Zaidel, head of the project. 'The rules that apply to word recognition in general do not necessarily apply here'. The study confirmed that brand names engage the 'emotional' right-brain more than other words. A London brand strategist told the magazine 'This is very intriguing indeed. It supports our instinctive belief that brands are a special class of word – they are like a poem all in one word in their ability to evoke and express ideas.'

CONFUCIUS

Lead the people with governmental measures and regulate them by law and punishments, and they will avoid wrongdoing, but will have no sense of honour and shame. Lead them by virtue and regulate them by the rules of propriety and they will have a sense of shame and, moreover, set themselves right.

Confucius, *The Analects*, 2:3

The great sage of the sixth century BC is also recorded as saying: 'I transmit rather than create'.

According to William P Alford, author of *To Steal a Book is an Elegant Offence*, the attitudes enshrined in these aphorisms had a determining effect on the Chinese attitude to intellectual property. Until the country opened itself to Western influence in the early twentieth century, its intellectual property system was effectively self-regulating, relying on the principles of respect and tradition.

PARADISE GIVEN-AWAY-FOR-EIGHTEEN-QUID

The Restoration (1660), when Charles II returned from exile to re-establish the British monarchy, was bad news for the great poet John Milton. He had previously written pamphlets defending the execution of the king's father. Milton fell on hard times and lost his sight into the bargain. In 1665 he completed his masterpiece *Paradise Lost*, and two years later he sold the copyright to Samuel Simmons, a London bookseller, for 10 pounds (five up front plus five for first three subsequent editions). When Milton died in 1674, his widow sold Simmons the remaining rights for another eight pounds.

Paradise Lost went on to become one of the best-selling works in history.

ACCIDENTAL INVENTIONS

The Microwave Oven

In 1946, Percy Le Baron Spencer, a war hero and electronics expert at the Raytheon Company, was working on a radar device called a magnetron. Suddenly he noticed a strange sensation in his pocket. On examination, he found that the chocolate bar he had secreted there earlier had started to melt. Instead of panicking, Spencer rushed out to get some corn kernels. Then he held the paper bag in front of the magnetron and listened in satisfaction as the corn began to pop. After further experiments with food, he realised he had a new form of oven on his hands.

The Raytheon Corporation produced the first commercial microwave oven in 1954. The 1161 Radarange was the size of a fridge and weighed 750 pounds. It would take Amana (a division of Raytheon) 13 years to come up with a viable domestic version.

Percy Spencer died in 1970. During his lifetime, he held more than 120 patents.

TRADEMARKS IN THE ANCIENT WORLD

5000 BC	Cave paintings show bison with symbols on their flanks.
3500 BC	Cylindrical seals are used in Mesopotamian to identify the provenance of goods. Analagous stone seals in Knossos, Crete.
3000 BC	'Trademarks' start to appear Egypt during the First Dynasty
2000 BC	Potters' seals are used near Corinth.
Roman era	Bricks are regularly stamped to indicate their manufacturer.

MICHAEL JACKSON OWNS...

Fifty per cent of the publishing rights to more than 250 Beatles songs (but not to the first two singles, *Love Me Do/PS I Love You* and *Please Please Me/Ask Me Why*, which were published before the formation of Northern Songs and are now owned by Paul McCartney's MPL Communications).

Jackson purchased the Northern Songs Catalogue from Lew Grade's ATV Music Publishing in 1985 for a reported US$47 million. In 1995, he merged the company with Sony's music publishing arm to form Sony/ATV. Jacko's stake was valued at US$450 million in 2003.

THE GREAT INVENTORS

Benjamin Franklin

Although he is perhaps best remembered as a statesman, having contributed to the drafting of the American Declaration of Independence and been instrumental in persuading the French to side with the colony against the British, Benjamin Franklin was most famous during his lifetime for his numerous inventions.

1717 Invents a pair of manually operated swim fins.

1751 *Experiments and Observations on Electricity* is published in London.

1752 Franklin conducts his seminal kite flying experiments in a series of thunder storms. At considerable personal risk, he proves that lightning is a form of electricity. The first lightening conductors appear on the market shortly afterwards.

1752 While serving as Postmaster General, Franklin invents a simple odometer to calculate the distances of postal routes.

1752 To help his ailing brother Franklin invented a urinary catheter, which improved upon previous models.

c. 1761 Franklin invents a glass armonica. He later said of the instrument 'Of all my inventions, the glass armonica has given me the greatest personal satisfaction.'

1783 Franklin observes the world's first manned balloon flight in Paris. When a fellow spectator questions the utility of the new invention, he remarks 'Of what use is a new born baby?'

c. 1784 Franklin invents bifocal spectacles.

c. 1785 The ageing Franklin unveils an instrument for taking down books from high shelves.

QUOTE UNQUOTE

Genius is one per cent inspiration and ninety-nine per cent perspiration.
Thomas Alva Edison, US scientist and inventor

THE CAT IN THE HAT BITES BACK

When Penguin brought out a parody version of *Dr Seuss's Cat in the Hat,* in which a character named Dr Juice recounted the story of the OJ Simpson double murder case, Seuss Enterprises sued the publishers for copyright and trademark infringement and won on both counts.

The Solar Powered Torch

A fine example of a chindogu, *an 'unuseless' invention
of a kind popular in Japan. To qualify as a chindogu,
a device must 'work' but be useless in practice. They
are therefore unpatentable by definition.*

Another Chindogu

*Why waste time sweeping the floor when you can get a
crawling baby to do it for you? Just slip your tot into the
dual purpose garment illustrated above and Hey Presto!*

CLASSICAL INSPIRATION

**Link up the modern song with the piece of
classical music on which it is based:**

a) *Russians* – Sting
b) *Lady Linda* – The Beach Boys
c) *Emerald City* – The Seekers
d) *Altogether Now* – The Farm
e) *If I Had Words* – Scott Fitzgerald and Yvonne Keely
f) *All By Myself* – Eric Carmen

1) Saint-Saens – *The Organ Symphony*
2) Prokofiev – *Lieutenant Kije*
3) Rachmaninoff – *Piano Concerto No.2*
4) Pachelbel – *Canon*
5) JS Bach – *Jesu Joy of Man's Desiring*
6) Beethoven – *9th Symphony*

Answer on page 153.

QUOTE UNQUOTE

*Diana basically right now is a cottage industry in the United States.
She is worth the economy of a small Third World nation.*
Alicia Mundy of *Adweek* magazine to BBC TV's *Panorama* in 1998

THOUGHT LEADERS:
PATENTS THAT HAVE CHANGED THE WORLD

Aryloxphenylpropylamines (otherwise known as Prozac)
US Patent No. 4,314,081

Few breakthroughs have been attended by as much controversy as Prozac: it seem you either love it or hate it. Whatever your view of its therapeutic value, there is no denying the power of this pharmaceutical product to transform the lives of depression sufferers.

Behind this breakthrough was a team at Eli Lilly, including Klaus Schmeigel and Bryan Molloy, who co-invented a class of aryloxphenylpropylamines. This class included fluexetine hydrochloride, for which Prozac is the registered Prozac name. Now the most pre-scribed anti-depressant in the US, Prozac received its patent in February 1982 and went on the market in the US in February 1988. It gained its 'most pre-scribed' status in a mere two years. Prozac was the first product in a class of drugs intended to treat depression, called 'selective serotonin re-uptake inhibitors'. The drug achieves its affect by increasing brain levels of the neurotransmitter serotonin, although the exact reason that this alleviates the effects of depression are not known.

ORIGIN OF THE NAME

NERF

NERF is a plastic foam material invented in 1968 and used to make child-friendly toys. Just as importantly, they are also adult-friendly – NERF products are virtually incapable of damaging furniture. Parker Brothers Inc. (later acquired by Hasbro) brought out the Nerf-ball in 1969 and had sold four million within 12 months. Four years later, the NERF soccer ball appeared and went on to become the world's best-selling indoor football. The product has since been used to make all manner of toys, notably a range of harmless weaponry.

The point of this story is that, as far as anyone can establish, 'NERF' doesn't stand for anything.

'A PATENT OF THE HEART'

Hope is a strange invention –
A Patent of the Heart –
In unremitting action
Yet never wearing out –

Of this electric Adjunct
Not anything is known
But its unique momentum
Embellish all we own –
Emily Dickinson, 'Hope is a strange invention'

THE FIRST WORLD FAIR

The first World Fair was the Great Exhibition of 1851. It set the standard for exhibitions the world over – not least as the perfect place to showcase new inventions, such as the sewing machine and the world's first set of false teeth.

The organisers, including Prince Albert, hoped it would be a celebration of modern industrial technology and design. It was certainly a celebration of modern architecture; it was housed in a gigantic glasshouse in Hyde Park, designed by Paxton, and dubbed 'The Crystal Palace'.

As an endorsement of nineteenth-century free trade, the Fair was certainly a success. It welcomed 13,000 exhibitors from all over the world, and was visited by six million people. Indeed, its profits were such that the money was used to found several museums in London including the Victoria and Albert Museum, the Science Museum and the Natural History Museum. After the Fair closed, The Crystal Palace was moved to Sydenham and part of London was named after its new structure. Unfortunately, the structure no longer survives.

USELESS PATENTS

The 'Amphibious Sulky Single Horse-drawn Light Vehicle'
Or, the 'horse-drawn' boat to you and me.

FR patent no. 2,694,256 – patented as recently as 1994 – provides the perfect means of travelling from a to b for those who just can't bear to leave their horses behind. Constructed using a harness attached to the horse, this vehicle requires the horse to plunge into the water and swim his passengers to their destinations.

DECIPHER THE TRADEMARK

The following is the official description of a registered US trademark associated with which legendary figure? You may want to get out your piano...

'A yell consisting of a series of approximately 10 alternating between the chest and falsetto registers of the voice, as follow – 1) a semi-long sound in the chest register, 2) a short sound up an interval of one octave plus a fifth from the preceding sound, 3) a short sound down a Major 3rd from the preceding sound, 4) a short sound up a Major 3rd from the preceding sound, 5) a long sound down one octave plus a Major 3rd from the preceding sound, 6) a short sound up one octave from the preceding sound, 7) a short sound up a Major 3rd from the preceding sound, 8) a short sound down a Major 3rd from the preceding sound, 9) a short sound up a Major 3rd from the preceding sound, 10) a long sound down an octave plus a fifth from the preceding sound.'

Answer on page 153.

NUMBERS BETWEEN 1 AND 100 AVAILABLE AS TRADEMARKS*

If you want a snappy new trademark, consider this. As of February 2004, all these numbers were still up for grabs at the United States Patent and Trademark Office, ie not registered in stand-alone form:

16, 26, 27, 28, 34, 36, 41, 42, 46, 49, 52, 54, 55, 58, 59, 60, 61, 62, 64, 65, 66, 68, 70, 71, 72, 73, 74, 78, 79, 81, 83, 85, 86, 89, 93, 94, 95, 96 and 97.

* To qualify for the list of numbers that are registered as trademarks, the officially registered word mark of a service or product must consist only one of the digit(s) in question.

All the riches of English literature are ours. English authorship comes to us free as the vital air, untaxed, unhindered, even by the necessity of translation, into the country; and the question is, shall we tax it, and thus impose a barrier to the circulation of intellectual and moral light? Shall we build up a dam to obstruct the flow of the rivers of knowledge?

Letter from the publishers Sherman and Jackson to the US Senate and House of Representatives, 1842

In this context, 'untaxed' means 'copyright-free'. The publishers were vehemently opposed to proposals for the US to sign up to an international copyright agreement. They were making a tidy sum from the unlicensed reproduction of British works and didn't fancy paying for the privilege.

LANDMARKS IN THE HISTORY OF GENETIC PATENTS

In 1998, developmental biologist Stuart Newman applied for a patent on a process to produce a 'chimerical' creature. Newman had no intention of actually making the part-human, part-animal monster – he just wanted to spark public debate. But in 1999 the United States Patent and Trademark Office (USPTO) rejected his application due to the human component of the invention. Newman announced his attention to appeal, if necessary all the way up to the Supreme Court. In 2004, he was reportedly still locked in a legal battle with the USPTO.

SEVEN RIDICULOUSLY LONG DOMAIN NAMES

http://www.thelongestdomainnameintheworldandthensomeandthensomemoreandmore.com

http://www.aaaaaaaaaaaaaaaaaaaaaaaaaaaaaaaaaaaaaaaaaaaaaaaaaaaaaaaaa.com/

http://www.llanfairpwllgwyngyllgogerychwyrndrobwyll-llantysiliogogogoch.com

http://www.thepersonwithanewideaisacrank-untiltheideasucceeds-by-marktwain.com/

http://abcdefghijklmnopqrstuvwxyzabcdefghijklmnopqrstuvwxyzabcdefghijk.com

http://www.buecher-und-verlage-verlagswesen-belletristik-und-sachbuecher.de/

http://www.modestapparelchristianclothinglydiaofpurpledressescustomsewing.com/

Vaseline

Robert Chesebrough was an enterprising young kerosene salesman who fell on hard times when his supply of sperm whale oil dried up. So in 1859, he went to seek his fortune in the oilfields of Pennsylvania. His quest turned out to be successful, but not in a way anyone could have imagined. Soon after his arrival, Chesebrough noticed the oil workers complaining about something they called 'rod wax'. This was a waxy substance that formed on their drilling equipment and gummed it up. Its only redeeming feature as far as they were concerned was its ability to speed up the healing of small cuts and bruises.

Intrigued, Chesebrough took a sample of 'rod wax' back to his laboratory in Brooklyn. Eventually, he worked out how to isolate the substance from ordinary petroleum. Then he started to experiment with it, subjecting himself to all manner of cuts and burns before applying the petroleum jelly. Everything healed magnificently.

To popularise his invention, Chesebrough gave it the name 'Vaseline' (from *wasser*, the German for water and *elaion*, Greek for oil). Then he embarked on a singularly masochistic road show, demonstrating his faith in his product by wounding himself in public before applying it. Soon he was selling a jar a minute. His customers used Vaseline for every conceivable purpose from clearing nasal congestion to cleaning furniture. By the end of the nineteenth century, Chesebrough was extremely rich and his petroleum jelly was breaking into Europe.

Chesebrough persisted with his 'practice what you preach' attitude toward Vaseline throughout his life. Shortly before he died at the impressive age of 96, he revealed that he had been eating a spoonful of the stuff every day for many years.

WELL IT SEEMED LIKE A GOOD IDEA AT THE TIME

Peter Blake, who designed the cover of the Beatles' album *Sgt Pepper's Lonely Hearts Club Band*, sold the rights for £200. Had he kept them, he would of course have collected royalties every time the album was sold.

Hilda Brabban, the creator of the 1960s children's television characters Bill and Ben, fared even worse. She simply gave her rights to the BBC, which has since earned more than two million pounds from videos and other Bill and Ben merchandise.

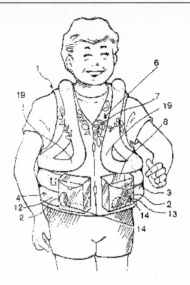

US Patent No. 5,901,666
Issued: May 11, 1999
Inventor: Brice Belisle

An important development for those reluctant to conceal their rodents or other small animals in their pockets. The lucky hammy or gerbil is free to gallivant through the attached transparent tunnels, doubtless to the delight of passers by.

ORIGIN OF THE NAME

Häagen-Dazs

Reuben Mattus started working for his mother's New York-based ice-cream business in the early 1920s. He sold her wares in the Bronx from a horse drawn wagon. Mattus was a bit of a visionary and dreamed of creating the world's best ice-cream. As a result of his business acumen and insistence on the use of top quality ingredients, the company expanded considerably during the 1930s, 1940s and 1950s.

In 1961, Reuben decided to go it alone. To give the new brand an air of old fashioned European know-how, he dreamed up the name Häagen-Dazs.

US CITIES BY NUMBER OF DESIGN PATENTS
GRANTED TO 'INDEPENDENT' INDIVIDUALS

Sheboygan, Wisconsin and Portland, Oregon may be the hotbeds of American design in corporate terms, but if only independent inventors are considered, a different pattern emerges:

Metro Area	Design pats granted	Population (1998)	Pats per 100,000
Reno, NV	19	313,660	6.1
Sharon, PA	7	121,938	5.7
Ventura, CA	36	731,967	4.9
Chico-Paradise, CA	9	194,597	4.6
Orange County, CA	123	2,721,701	4.5
Los Angeles – Long Beach, CA	378	9,213,533	4.1
Santa Barbara, CA	16	389,502	4.1
Naples, FL	8	199,436	4.0
Newark, NJ	65	1,952,407	3.3
Parkersberg-Marietta, WV/OH	5	150,181	3.3

Source: United States Patent and Trademark Office

QUOTE UNQUOTE

The human body is a magazine of inventions, the patent office, where are the models from which every hint is taken. All the tools and engines on earth are only extensions of its limbs and senses.
Ralph Waldo Emerson, US philosopher and essayist

PRINCESS DI P

'These letters were private. They were written by the Duke of Edinburgh to the Princess of Wales. At no stage were they written to her butler and there is no evidence that she bequeathed them to him. They were written by a concerned father-in-law to his daughter-in-law at a difficult time. It is appalling that somebody is using them simply to make money. They are not, and never were, his intellectual property to use.'

Under UK law, the content of the letters was automatically copyrighted to the Duke when he committed it to writing.

220,000 The sum, in US dollars, that an anonymous English businessman lost, after receiving an email requesting help transferring US$12 million, from someone he describes as a 'respectable sounding businessman called Vincent'.

94 The number of respondents in a British national consumer's opinion poll who said they'd received unsolicited emails offering financial service or money-making schemes.

50 million The number of songs – at 99 cents per track – legally downloaded from Apple's online music store iTunes since its launch in April 2003.

335 million The number of times file sharers have downloaded the latest version of KaZaA, the peer to peer network that allows copyright-protected music to be exchanged online without charge.

83 The percentage of UK companies who have been victims of computer crime; 17% of which involved financial crimes that cost companies £121 million (US $219 million) in 2003, according to a National Hi-Tech Crime Unit survey.

917 million The number of listings for goods to sell on online market place eBay in 2003 – a 50% increase on 2002.

150,000 The sum, in US dollars, of charges that PayPal, eBay's online payments system has agreed to pay after an investigation by New York Attorney General Eliot Spitzer's office. PayPal was found to have misrepresented its services to 40 million account holders in its user agreement, when it stated that holders had 'the rights and privileges expected of a credit card transaction.'

Sources: BBC, Consumer Affairs.com, eBay, Reuters, International Herald Tribune

VW BADGES AND THE BEASTIES

In 1986, US rappers The Beastie Boys started to appear on stage with Volkswagen badges around their necks. This unlikely fashion statement sparked a mini crime-wave. Fans throughout the world descended on parked Golfs and Polos and prised off the coveted 'VW' badges with screwdrivers. Then they strung them and wore them as pendants, thus aping their heroes and demonstrating their fearless street nous.

The manufacturers responded by ordering up enough replacement badges to fill a room four-feet wide by eight-feet deep.

Although the craze eventually died down, a spate of VW badge theft was reported in Yorkshire as late as 2000.

Number of utility patents awarded to the Massachusetts Institute of 127 Technology in 2003

Unfortunately for the human race, when old Ma Necessity takes a day off, her dim cousin Utter Pointlessness takes over.

QUOTE UNQUOTE

Self-plagiarism is style.
Alfred Hitchcock, film director,
defending his repeated use of certain filming techniques.

AN UNWISE MOVE

In 1996, The American Society of Composers, Authors, and Publishers (ASCAP) came very close to suing the Girl Scouts for singing 'Row, Row, Row Your Boat' around the campfire. In the end, a blizzard of negative publicity persuaded ASCAP to relent.

THOUGHT LEADERS:
PATENTS THAT HAVE CHANGED THE WORLD.

The Automatic Teller Machine *US Patent No. 3,761,682*

Few inventions have been as convenient to use as the Automatic Teller Machine (ATM). The first ATM was installed outside Chemical Bank in New York in 1969 – at a cost of almost US$30,000. Now more than 1.2 million are installed around the world and according to a recent survey in the US 54% of the population are using them.

Don Wetzel, the ATM's chief inventor came up with the idea while standing in a queue at his local bank. Wetzel, who worked for Docutel, a company that produced automated baggage handling equipment, formed a team with co-inventors Tom Barnes as George Chastain. Five years (and five million dollars) later in 1973, Docutel was issued the patent for 'a currency dispenser (that) automatically delivers a medium of exchange in packets in response to a coded credit card presented thereto'.

The significance of Docutel's invention is that it relied on credit cards with magnetic strips and personal ID numbers to extract cash. Previously patents had been issued for machines that delivered cash and machines that enabled customers to pay bills without visiting a teller and in 1967 Barclays Bank installed a cash dispenser in one of its London branches that required customers to insert paper vouchers bought from tellers in advance.

Despite bankers' initial reluctance over high costs, and customer wariness – which some banks resolved by giving away ice creams to ATM customers – the ATM quickly took off and by 1973 there were 2,000 ATMs in the US. Last year in the UK 2,268 million withdrawals were made from 40,825 ATMs across the country. In just 30 years the ATM has revolutionised the banking industry – eliminating long lines on pay-day and enabling customers to withdraw money at any time, from almost anywhere in the world.

ART AND 'THOU SHALT NOT STEAL'

Nothing is sillier than this charge of plagiarism. There is no sixth commandment in art. The poet dare help himself wherever he lists, wherever he finds material suited to his work. He may even appropriate entire columns with their carved capitals, if the temple he thus supports be a beautiful one. Goethe understood this very well, and so did Shakespeare before him.

Heinrich Heine

MR LEGOLAND WINDSOR

In 2000, Craig Cottrell from the royal town of Windsor got into a drinking session with a friend in a local pub. Several pints later, the two struck a £50 bet. To win, Cottrell had to change his name by deed poll to 'Legoland Windsor'. His mate, meanwhile, had to register as 'Cadbury's Chocolate'.

In the event, only Mr Cottrell went through with the plan and he duly collected his 50 quid. He also registered the domain name legolandwindsor.com as his personal website. To no one's surprise, this failed to impress the Danish toy manufacturing giant Lego, which owned a theme park outside Windsor also called Legoland. Lego commenced legal proceedings, and in August the High Court ordered Cottrell to hand over the URL to the Danes. But he refused to respond to the official letters, arguing that they were 'addressed to Craig Cottrell, not me'.

In 2001, it emerged that Cottrell's antics had been motivated by more than drunken impetuousness. In February of that year, he was sentenced to a year's imprisonment for using bogus websites named after famous companies to extract credit card details from unsuspecting surfers.

IGNORING A FIFTH OF THE WORLD'S POPULATION

Histories of the world omitted China; if a Chinaman invented compass or movable type or gunpowder we promptly 'forgot it' and named their European inventors. In short, we regarded China as a sort of different and quite inconsequential planet.
    WEB du Bois, US writer and social reformer, writing in 1912

FOOTBALLERS AND INTELLECTUAL PROPERTY

In 2003, the England manager Sven-Goran Eriksson successfully registered his name as a UK trademark. The registration covered a spectrum of potential products, from hair lotions, soaps and sporting articles to medical services, non-alcoholic drinks and milk products. The wisdom of the move depends on success on the pitch: if England win the World Cup in 2006, there may well be a demand for Sven Goran Eriksson rubber goods.

The relevant applications were conducted through Mr Eriksson's agent, the splendidly named Athole Still. You never know, Mr Still might find commercial use for his own name one day.

WAL-MART BY NUMBERS

Fast stats on the world's largest supermarket

41 The age in years of the US grocery giant. It was founded by Sam Walton, whose heirs own about 38% of the company.

64% Percentage of consumers polled in a brand recognition survey conducted by US firm Emergence in July 2003 who identified Wal-mart's slogan 'Always low prices. Always.'

$1.42 billion The sum, in US dollars, that Wal-mart recently made in sales during one day's trading; bigger than the annual GDP of 36 countries.

1 Wal-mart's position in the ranking for the largest companies in the world. It is three times the size of the number two retailer; France's Carrefour.

2 billion The estimated sum, in US dollars, that Wal-mart loses through theft each year. If this amount were incorporated as a business it would rank No. 694 on the Fortune 1,000.

5,200 The number of stores Walmart owns around the world – 3,400 in the US and 1,200 overseas in nine countries including Canada, Mexico, South America, Europe and Asia.

82 The percentage of American households who made at least one purchase at Wal-mart in 2002.

30,000 The number of Wal-mart trucks that have its slogan 'Always low prices. Always' painted on the side.

1972 The year Wal-mart was listed on the stock exchange.

138 million the number of shoppers who visit a Wal-mart store at least once a week.

30% Percentage market share Wal-mart commands in America for household staples, such as toothpaste, shampoo, and paper towels.

20 billion The sum, in US dollars, that New England consulting estimates Wal-mart saved its customers in cost efficiencies in 2002.

1.3 million the number of employees who work for Wal-mart worldwide.

400 The number of ex-employees who claimed they had been forced to work unpaid overtime between 1994 and 1999 and won a class action lawsuit against the global supermarket giant in 2002.

600 billion The sum, in US dollars, that Wal-mart is estimated to make in 2011 if it continues its current 15% growth rate. Its revenues in 2002 were US$245 billion.

234,329 The number of people who have visited www.walmartsurvivor.com since the website was set up on 14 October 1999

Sources: Fortune, BBC News, CBS News, The International Herald Tribune

The parties are advised to chill.
Circuit Judge Alex Kozinski, July 2002. The parties in question were MCA Records and Mattel Inc, manufacturers of the Barbie Doll. Mattel had alleged that the song *Barbie Girl* by the Danish band Aqua infringed their trademark. Kozinski ruled in favour of MCA, but used this choice piece of legalese to dissuade the companies from pursuing their row in the media.

ACCIDENTAL INVENTIONS

The Pacemaker

It's comforting to know that even great inventors can get their wires crossed. They may get blown up, but on the other hand they may find they have stumbled on something truly useful.

During the late 1950s, Wilson Greatbatch, a University of Buffalo professor, was working with cardiologists to find a way to record human heart sounds. One day, while constructing an experimental machine for this purpose, he decided he needed to install a 10,000 ohm resistor (a current regulating device). Greatbatch reached into his tool box and inadvertently pulled out a 1,000,000 ohm resistor. It was an easy mistake to make – the colour codes on the tiny electrical components were almost identical: brown/black/orange for the type he was after, brown/black/green for the one he selected. Once he had installed the 'wrong' resistor, Greatbatch checked the circuit. There was a pulse, then a second's silence, then another pulse. It sounded just like a heartbeat. 'I said 'wait a minute – this is a pacemaker!" the inventor later recalled.

The next task was to shrink the new machine to manageable proportions. So Greatbatch settled down in an old barn 'to solve the problem how to reduce an electronic apparatus in the size of a kitchen cabinet to the size of a baby's hand, in order to be able to be able to implant this pacemaker into the chest'. Within two years, he had come up with the world's first implantable cardiac pacemaker. He filed a US patent application for the device on July 22, 1960. Then, to complete the job, he invented a non-corrosive lithium battery to power it.

Greatbatch, who was born in 1919 and has been awarded more than 150 American patents, was inducted into the Inventors' Hall of Fame in 1986. His pacemaker has prolonged the lives of millions, including Dick Cheney and Mother Teresa.

IS IT A BIRD?

The last recorded words of inventor Ivor Nydear: 'I can't believe no one patented this before.'

WORD PUZZLE

Decipher this clue to reveal a venerable British trademark:

R

LAND

Answer on page 153.

CHINDOGU

'Chindogu' literally means 'weird tool'. The term was coined by Japanese inventor Kenji Kawakami to denote a particular species of gadget he was fond of making. To qualify as a chindogu, an invention has to possess the elusive quality of 'unuselessness'. In other words, it has to work in theory but be thoroughly impractical. Examples of the genre include a combined duster/cocktail-shaker for the housewife who likes to mix business with pleasure, the all-over plastic bathing costume for hydrophobes, and the all-day tissue dispenser for people prone to hay-fever (essentially a toilet roll built into a hat).

Kawakami sees a spiritual purpose in this cult artform. For him, chingdogus are 'invention dropouts' that have escaped 'the suffocating historical dominance of conservative utility.' To preserve the integrity of the form, he has issued a 10-point checklist.

1. A chindogu cannot be for real use. If it works too successfully, you've failed.

2. It must exist – you have to actually make your contraption.

3. The spirit of anarchy is essential to a good chindogu.

4. Chindogu are tools for every day life.

5. They must never be sold, even in jest.

6. Your device must solve a real problem, but preferably one so minor that no one has worried much in its absence.

7. Chindogu must never be created to make profound comments on the human condition.

8. Chindogu must never break taboos or normal standards of decency.

9. Chindogu must not be patented. For one thing, this would mean that they were too useful, for another they should be viewed as free gifts to the world.

10. Chindogu do not favour some sections of the population at the expense of others. Everyone must be free to un-use them.

CELEBRITY INVENTORS

Abraham Lincoln

In 1849, future president Abraham patented not the stovepipe hat or his distinctive beard arrangement, but 'a manner of buoying vessels' (US patent no. 6,469). At the time, he was still an Illinois congressman. The invention was never taken up commercially, but there is a wooden model in the Smithsonian Institution in Washington DC.

QUOTE UNQUOTE

If you steal from one author, it's plagiarism;
if you steal from many, it's research.
Wilson Mizner, screenwriter

MOST VALUABLE BRANDS ON EARTH 2004

Coca-Cola	US$67.39 billion
Microsoft	US$61.37 billion
IBM	US$53.79 billion
GE	US$44.11 billion
Intel	US$33.50 billion
Disney	US$27.11 billion
McDonald's	US$25.00 billion
Nokia	US$24.04 billion
Toyota	US$22.67 billion
Marlboro	US$22.13 billion

Source: Interbrand and Business Week

THOUGHT LEADERS:
PATENTS THAT HAVE MADE A DIFFERENCE.

Adrenalin *Patent No. 4785*
The Japanese chemist Jokichi Takamine is credited with being the first to isolate and purify a human hormone. In 1901, he successfully isolated the crystalline hormone adrenalin (epinephrine), making commercial preparation possible. He obtained patent rights to the manufacturing method he invented. Epinephrine is used to treat symptoms of cardiac arrest, the treatment of shock, asthma and glaucoma.

FIRST US 'RIGHT OF PUBLICITY' CASE

In 1935, Hanna Manufacturing Co sued Hillerich & Bradsbury Co for using the names, signatures and photographs of famous baseball players to which it claimed exclusive rights, specifically in connection with the sale and advertising of baseball bats. A district court ruled in favour of Hanna, thereby setting a precedent for the recognition of a 'Right of Publicity'. But the Court of Appeals reversed the decision, ruling that Hanna's contracts with the players covered only its own use of their names. The judgement declared that '[F]ame is not merchandise. It would help neither sportsmanship nor business to uphold the sale of a famous name to the highest bidder as property.' My, times have changed!

D'OH! GREAT MISSED
PATENTING OPPORTUNITIES

James Watson and Francis Crick – DNA molecule structure (discovered 1953)

Otto Titzling – Invented the bra in Paris in 1910 after hearing a well-endowed opera singer named Swanhilda Olafsen complain about the lack of support corsets gave to her bosom. In 1929, the French flying ace turned fashion designer Phillipe de Brassière got wind of Titzling's halter-like invention and glamourised it. Titzling (and no, we didn't make the name up) sued him for damages, but lost as he had omitted to file a patent.

11 CELEBRITIES PHOTOGRAPHED
DRINKING COCA COLA

The Beatles (that's four)
JFK
Elvis
Mae West
Grace Kelly
Marlon Brando
Jean Harlow
Fidel Castro (in a major coup for the company)

THE OLD HIPPY!

Although human subtlety makes a variety of inventions by different means to the same end, it will never devise an invention more beautiful, more simple or more direct than does nature because in her inventions nothing is lacking, and nothing is superfluous.

Leonardo da Vinci

COVERING UP

The cardigan is believed to have been invented by James Thomas Brudenell, the seventh Earl of Cardigan. Brudenell is most famous for leading his troops to slaughter in the disastrous Charge of the Light Brigade. But if fighting was not his forte, he was a dab hand with a pair of knitting needles. In addition to the eponymous woolly waistcoat, Brudenell is also thought to have invented the Balaclava, designed to protect his soldiers' faces from the bitter cold of the Crimean winter. It was first worn at the battle of Balaclava (1854), during which the infamous Charge took place.

On 16 October 2004, a Native American wearing a full ceremonial headdress walked up to the Crazy Horse strip club in Paris. But Alfred Red Cloud, a member of the Oglala Sioux tribe, hadn't travelled five thousand miles to ogle the girls. He was there to deliver a letter on behalf of his people asking the club's operators to change its 53-year-old name.

The author of the letter was Harvey White Woman, a descendent of the original Crazy Horse (a legendary Oglala warrior and key player in the Sioux Wars of the 1860s and 1870s) and an executor of his estate. He had been spurred into action by an HBO cable programme in which dancers from the Paris club were shown cavorting around in feathered headdresses. 'I want the young people of my tribe to remember him [Crazy Horse] as a strong leader and warrior and not some nightclub in Paris,' he wrote in the letter.

Outside the Crazy Horse Saloon, Alfred Red Cloud elaborated on the tribe's objections.

'The name is a sacred name to our people. Nobody uses that name back home – even our own people. I'm not trying to close the establishment down' he added, 'I just want the name changed'. He also admitted to being concerned about the club's politics. 'As I went into the place, the way it is set up, it exposes women,' he said. 'Women are sacred to us, they are the keepers of our generations to come.'

Although at the time of going to press it was unclear how the owners of the Parisian club intended to respond, they would be well advised to take note of a legal precedent. In 1992, the descendants of Crazy Horse sued Hornell Brewing Co of Brooklyn, New York, for marketing what it described as 'The Original Crazy Horse Malt Liquor'. The case was settled out of court with the company agreeing to drop the name and pay the family US$150,000 compensation.

It makes you wonder how Siouxsie and the Banshees ever got away with it.

SIX CANADIAN INVENTIONS

1. **Basketball** (James Naismith, 1892)
2. **Lightbulb** (Henry Woodward, 1874.
Edison's version was an 'improvement')
3. **Electron microscope**
(E Burton, C Hall, J Hillier, A Prebus, late 1930s)
4. **IMAX** (G Ferguson, R Kroitor, R Kerr, 1968)
5. **Paint Roller** (Norman Blakely, patented 1940)
6. **Snow-blower** (Arthur Siccard, 1927)

**The following sounds are registered as trademarks with the
United States Patent and Trademark Office:**

1. The NBC Chimes – the world's first registered sound mark, consisting of the notes G, E and C sounded in sequence in the key of C. The chimes pay tribute to the General Electric Company, one of the founders of NBC.
2. Sweet Georgia Brown – registered as a trademark of the Harlem Globetrotters.
3. The MGM Lion Roar.
4. Nine bars of primarily musical chords in the key of B Flat – Twentieth Century Fox Film Corporation.
5. The spoken term 'Cha-Ching' – owned by Rally's Hamburgers, Inc.
6. The words 'the dreams we share, we'll always remember, remember with the music of your life', set to music – radio jingle owned by Al Ham Productions.

And here are a couple from Australia:

1. The sound of the word 'sproing' pronounced such that there is initially a rise in pitch at the 'oi' sound, which is then substantially elongated and pronounced with vibrato on the 'oing' portion of the word, so as to imitate the sound of a spring reverberating on metal – owned by Pacific Brands Clothing Pty Ltd, manufacturers of floor coverings and underlay.
2. 'Yahoo', sung in a yodelling style – owned by Yahoo, Inc. (Delaware).

QUOTE UNQUOTE

*The greatest inventors are unknown to us.
Someone invented the wheel – but who?*
Isaac Asimov, science-fiction writer

DOO LANG DOO LANG MY LORD

In 1976, Bright Tunes Music Corp sued ex-Beatle George Harrison, alleging that his song *My Sweet Lord* (1970) infringed the copyright of The Chiffons' 1963 hit *He's So Fine*. Although the two songs were very different in feel, Harrison's being a hymn of praise to the Hindu god Krishna and The Chiffon's to a hunky US schoolboy, the resemblance was difficult to deny. Harrison claimed that he had not knowingly appropriated the melody in question, but although the court accepted this, it was deemed irrelevant. '[*My Sweet Lord*] is, under the law, infringement of copyright and is no less so even though subconsciously accomplished', was the landmark ruling.

In October 2002, the *Atlanta Journal-Constitution* received an unusual request from New York attorney Howard Siegel. Mr Siegel, representing Bill Wyman, the former Rolling Stones bassist, wanted the paper to run a disclaimer every time it printed the name of its music critic. The problem was that he also happened to be called Bill Wyman – although the letter demanded legal proof.

Wyman the journalist pointed out that he had been called 'Bill Wyman' for rather longer than Siegel's client, having been born in January 1961, two years before the bassist cashed in the name William George Perks for something more rock and roll. Nevertheless, he took the affair in good spirit, even suggesting a wording for the requested disclaimer ('Not that Bill Wyman').

In November 2002, Siegel sent an email to the *San Francisco Chronicle* to explain his rationale. 'No one should read an article on popular music,' he wrote, 'and on the Rolling Stones in particular, written by Bill Wyman, Charlie Watts, Mick Jagger or Keith Richards, believing he is therefore receiving information emanating from the "inside", only to realise that the author is not whom the reader thought it was.' But Siegel also indicated that the matter was now closed. 'Our request for a clarification has been largely accomplished, and with a reach and level of effectiveness well beyond that for which we might otherwise have hoped.'

SUCKS SUCKS

Jim Yagmin, a teenage former Kmart employee, sparked a major internet trend in 1995 when he set up a website to vent his spleen at his former bosses. 'Kmart sucks' was the first of a rash of unflattering domain names designed to get under the skins of large corporations and organisations. Kmart was distinctly unamused. Yagmin received a stiff letter from the company's lawyers, ordering him to '(1) Remove the icon "K" and any appearances of "K" with the likeness of that used by Kmart, including the red Kmart and the blue and gray Kmart sucks. (2) Remove the name Kmart from the "title" of any page. (3) At the bottom of "The Eternal Fear" page remove the lines "Go steal something from Kmart today, and tell em Punk God sent ya".' Yagmin responded by replacing the offending 'Ks' with 'Xs', but this failed to calm the nerves of his Internet Service Provider, which asked him to remove the site.

At the end of 1999, the US Congress put a stop to the 'sucks' malarkey by passing the Anti-Cyber Squatting Consumer Protection Act. This ensures penalties of up to US$100,000 for those using trademarked names in their domain names.

WHY IT'S GOOD TO FAIL

We learn wisdom from failure much more than from success; we often discover what will do, by finding out what will not do; and probably he who never made a mistake, never made a discovery. Horne Tooke used to say... that he had become all the better acquainted with the country, through having had the good-luck sometimes to lose his way. And a distinguished investigator in physical science has left it on record that, whenever in the course of his researches he encountered an apparently insuperable obstacle, he generally found himself on the brink of some novel discovery. The very greatest things – great thoughts, discoveries, inventions – have generally been nurtured in hardship, often pondered over in sorrow, and at length established with difficulty.

Samuel Smiles, Scottish author

LESSER-KNOWN COUNTRY CODES

To which countries do these domain-name suffixes belong?

.bn	.mg
.dj	.uy
.ee	.tt
.fk	.va
.ls	.za

Answer on page 153.

THE WRONG SPIRIT

On 5 March 1960, Alberto Gutierrez took one of the most iconic photographs of the twentieth century. The occasion was a memorial service in Havana for crew members of a Belgian arms cargo ship killed in an attack for which Cuba blamed counter-revolutionary forces aided by the US. The subject was Ernesto 'Che' Guevara.

Forty years later, Gutierrez, who goes by the professional name Alberta Korda, was surprised and furious to see his picture of Che in an advertisement for Smirnoff Vodka. 'To use the image of Che Guevara to sell vodka is a slur on his name and memory', he declared. 'He never drank himself, he was not a drunk and drink should not be associated with his immortal memory.' An organisation describing itself as the Cuba Solidarity Campaign filed a claim on his behalf at the High Court in London. It accused UK advertising agency Lowe Lintas and picture agency Rex Features of trivialising the photo's historical significance by combining it with a hammer and sickle motif with a chilli pepper substituted for the sickle. In 2000, Gutierrez/Korda accepted a substantial out of court settlement.

African Intellectual Property Organisation patent number for 'explosive compositions' (1966)

A BUSY FELLOW

Benjamin Franklin (1706–90) is most famous for flying a kite in a thunder storm, signing the American Declaration of Independence and inventing bifocal spectacles. But this only scratches the surface of his achievements. Franklin also:

1. Published almanacs
2. Was the first American ambassador
3. Invented the rocking chair
4. Came up with the idea of Daylight Saving Time
5. Introduced street-lamps
6. Invented the circulating library
7. Founded the Democratic Party
8. Organised the first city fire department
9. Was the father of modern dentistry

QUOTE UNQUOTE

I don't even know why I would want to be on a label in a few years, because I don't think it's going to work by labels and by distribution systems in the same way. The absolute transformation of everything that we ever thought about music will take place within 10 years, and nothing is going to be able to stop it. I see absolutely no point in pretending that it's not going to happen. I'm fully confident that copyright, for instance, will no longer exist in 10 years.
David Bowie in *The New York Times*, 2002

THE STATUE OF LIBERTY

What do you give a country for its 100th birthday? When the US reached its centenary in 1876, France decided that the obvious gift was a 151-foot/46.5-metre copper statue. The young French sculptor Auguste Bartholdi was commissioned to design the 225-tonne figure. According to legend, he based the face on his mother's and the body on that of a prostitute. It was left to the Americans to build a suitable pedestal.

As a result of fund shortages on both sides of the Atlantic, the project overran considerably. 'Liberty Enlightening the World' was finally unveiled, 10 years late, on Bedloe's Island in New York harbour on 15 October 1886.

Bartholdi was shrewd enough to secure a US design patent for his iconic creation (D11023, registered 18 February 1879).

'Happy birthday to you' must be sung more often than any other song in the world. It has even been performed in space. Yet bizarrely, the urban myth that *Happy Birthday to You* is protected by copyright is 100% accurate. Indeed, if current legislation continues to apply, it will remain protected in the USA until 2030.

The song that would become *Happy Birthday* was written by two sisters from Kentucky. Patty Smith Hill, born in 1868, was an influential educator who developed the 'Patty Hill blocks' used in schools throughout the US. Mildred J Hill (born 1859) started out as a kindergarten teacher but later developed into a composer. In the early 1890s, the sisters found themselves working at the same school. Mildred devised a simple melody for teachers to sing to their pupils at the beginning of lessons, and Patty added some child-friendly lyrics. *Good Morning to All* ran as follows:

> *Good morning to you,*
> *Good morning to you,*
> *Good morning, dear children,*
> *Good morning to all.*

In 1893, the song was published in *Song Stories for the Kindergarten*. The Happy Birthday lyric first appeared in print in 1924 in a songbook edited by Robert H Coleman. Initially included as an optional second verse, the new version rapidly took over from the original. This process was greatly facilitated by the media adopting *Happy Birthday* en masse. In 1931, for example, the song cropped up in the Broadway musical *The Band Wagon*, and two years later it was used for Western Union's first 'singing telegram'.

Back in Kentucky, a third Hill sister, Jessica, grew increasingly irritated by this unlicensed 'hijacking' of Patty and Mildred's song. The final straw was the melody's appearance in Irving Berlin's musical *As Thousands Cheer*. Jessica filed suit, and secured the rights for *Happy Birthday to You* for her sisters. In 1935, the Chicago-based Clayton F Summy Company published and copyrighted the song on the sisters' behalf.

Had the law remained unchanged, the copyright would have expired in 1991 (one 28-year term followed by a 28-year renewal), but as a result of the US Copyright Act (1976) and Copyright Term Extension Act (1998), *Happy Birthday* will remain protected until 2030. The rights to the song are currently owned by Summy-Birchard Music, a division of AOL Time Warner. *Happy Birthday* brings in about $2 million in royalties every year and the proceeds are split between Summy-Birchard and the Hill Foundation.

In case you're quivering behind the sofa awaiting prosecution for a lifetime of unlicensed Happy Birthday *singing, we should point out that you are not infringing copyright if you sing the song in private.*

ELECTRIFIED TABLE CLOTH

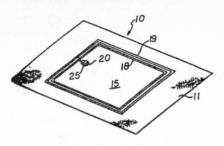

If you don't mind your meals punctuated by the odd buzz, this electrified tablecloth is just the thing for al fresco dining, particularly in the tropics. Any ant, termite or other crawling insect foolish enough to venture up your table legs will be swiftly dispatched, to the accompaniment of a small blue flash.
(US Patent No. 5,107,620)

THE APPLE B.H.A

In 1994, the astronomer Carl Sagan sued Apple Computer Inc for using his surname as an internal code word for the Power Macintosh 7100 during the product's development. What really irked him was the company's decision to switch to the name 'BHA' following his initial complaint. The media reported that the initials stood for 'Butt-Headed Astronomer', a claim a company spokesman declined to refute in court. Apple settled out of court in 1995.

FOOTBALLERS AND INTELLECTUAL PROPERTY

Towards the end of David Beckham's Manchester United career, the club was allegedly paying him £33,300 a week for the use of his image on club merchandise. Apart from this, he was free to choose his own endorsements. He did this in a big way, securing lucrative contracts with (among others) Brylcreem, Adidas and Police Sunglasses. But it was all change when he moved to Real Madrid. As top club official Emile Butragueno confirmed, 'When a player signs for Real Madrid he must give up his image rights for the club to manage.... This is a must, a policy of the club, but of course we would respect previous agreements.' Henceforward, Real would manage all Beckham's new image contracts, splitting the income 50-50 with 'Goldenballs'.

THE TRUE FACTS

It has been estimated by FACT that film piracy in the United Kingdom cost the UK film/video distributors and the retail sector a combined loss of £400 million in 2002 or, in terms of actual sales, a piracy infiltration rate of between 20% and 30%... That is, potentially 3 in every 10 videos purchased in the UK is an unauthorised copy obtained at markets, boot fairs and over the Internet. The sale of 'all branded goods' costs UK industry £1 billion and that causes immense damage to the legitimate industry and represents a huge loss to the exchequer.

It is known that organised crime has now taken up film piracy as an effective means of generating funds for other serious criminal activity and for laundering money... The Asia Pacific region predominantly Malaysia, Taiwan and Thailand, along with Pakistan, are global centres of illicit production and exportation of counterfeit DVD film media. The method of importation into the UK is, on the whole, via airfreight parcels with optical discs easily secreted and packed in bulk.

The industry is also starting to suffer significantly through 'commercial copying facilities' resulting in sales of CD and DVD-R product via the Internet or at markets and boot fairs. These facilities would invariably be found on small industrial units and home set-ups. Banks of CD/DVD 'burners' and videocassette recorders are able to produce thousand of units with the price for blank media falling significantly in recent years; this provides a real attraction to would be video pirates in terms of the potential financial return for a low start up and production cost.

As Broadband becomes more available to UK consumers, so we are experiencing more cases of pre-theatrical/video release film downloading and media file exchanges of films on the Internet.

Federation Against Copyright Theft (FACT) press release

BUILDING SHAPES AS TRADEMARKS

If the shape of a building is distinctive enough, the United States Patent and Trademark Office is often prepared to register it as a trademark. Here are a few examples:

1. The Transamerica Pyramid in San Francisco
2. The Guggenheim Museum
3. The Chrysler Building – both in New York City
4. The Citicorp Centre
5. The Wrigley Building – both in Chicago
6. The Rock and Roll Hall of Fame building in Cleveland, Ohio.

The shape (and colour) of McDonald's' golden arches is also a registered trademark.

PRINCESS DI P

By the time Princess Diana's childhood home, Althorp Park, was opened to the public in July 1999, her memorial fund was already under criticism for licensing her name to commercial enterprises deemed 'unsuitable' in some quarters. Examples included the Princess Beanie Baby and its follow up the Princess Beanie Buddy, a millennium wall calendar, lottery scratch-cards and Flora margarine. Cartons of the latter had appeared in shops bearing Diana's signature within seven months of her death.

Diana's trustees found themselves in a tricky situation. On the one hand, the trust had a moral duty to raise money for charity (and had raised an impressive $76 million by June 1998); on the other, the public tended to come over all snobbish whenever Diana's name was linked with down-to-earth products. This was ironic, as the 'People's Princess' was notoriously unstuffy, taking her children to theme parks and wolfing down burgers.

5 MOST FAKED BRANDS IN RUSSIA

According to polls conducted by Interactive Research Group in 2003, the faked brands most often encountered by shoppers in Moscow and the provincial Russian city of Samara were:

Adidas
Nike
Reebok
Kristal
Nescafé

A SMILEY CHARACTER

When the State Mutual Life Assurance Company of Worcester, Massachusetts, merged with the Guarantee Mutual Company of Ohio in the early 1960s, staff morale plummeted. To boost it, the company enlisted a graphic designer named Harvey Ball to come up with a perky symbol for use on company stationary. Within 10 minutes, he had produced a yellow, noseless, grinning circle, for which he was paid 45 dollars. The Smiley symbol would go on to became an icon of the hippie era and, a generation later, the international rave scene.

Over 50 million Smiley buttons had been sold by 1971, but Ball never received another cent. Nevertheless, he remained true to the spirit of his design. 'Hey, I can only eat one steak at a time', he would observe philosophically. Ball died in 2001.

ACCIDENTAL INVENTIONS

NutraSweet (or aspartame)

In 1965, Dr James Schlatter, a chemist at the GD Searle Company, was working to develop a new drug for the treatment of ulcers when he accidentally spilled some on his hand. When he licked his fingers, he noticed that the substance tasted sweet. In fact on analysis, it turned out to be 200 times sweeter than sugar. It also had virtually no calories and lacked the bitter aftertaste associated with many artificial sweeteners.

It took 16 years for Searle to win FDA approval to market aspartame, or NutraSweet as the giant drug company named the product, but before long, sales were in excess of US$1billion a year.

ANOTHER CRYPTIC INVENTOR

Who is the inventor?
MARC
I
Answer on page 153.

THE ART OF THE LOGO

The title of oldest trademark in the UK is held by Bass Breweries, whose distinctive red triangle motif is number one in the national trademark registry. It also features in Manet's Bar at the Folies Bergère (1882).

Crosse and Blackwell's logo has been in use since 1706, but the company didn't register it as a trademark until 1925.

THE SNOWBALLS CASE

Andy Goldsworthy, the internationally renowned artist and sculptor held two art exhibitions, one in Glasgow, and a second one actually in the streets of London, which featured giant snowballs with material embedded in them. The snowballs were left to melt in London during midsummer's day. The following year Habitat ran a poster campaign in London for their spring/summer catalogue featuring a giant melting snowball with two chairs embedded in the snowball. Mr Goldsworthy sued Habitat and their advertising agency for passing off and copyright infringement. The case was settled before trial with a payment of £70,000 and an apology from Habitat's advertising agency.

For an idea that does not at first seem insane, there is no hope.
Albert Einstein

IP BY NUMBERS

41
The number of licences granted by Acacia Research to the providers of interest streaming content. Acacia, which owns the patents to compressing and transferring streaming media files over the internet is currently negotiating with the major audio and video streaming providers on the internet.

1936
The year in which the red tag was added to the rear pocket of Levi's jeans, so that the brand could be easily identified from a distance. It is still easily spotted today.

521
The sum, in millions of US dollars, that Microsoft has been ordered to pay to software company Eolas after a court found Microsoft had infringed Eolas's patent which covers opening links to load a movie or video player through a web interface, such as Microsoft's Internet Explorer.

40
The number, in billions, of brown paper grocery bags used by Americans every year. The machine that made them was patented in 1882 by its inventor Charles Stillwell.

30
The number of minutes Wrigley's Viagra flavoured chewing gum should be chewed before it would take effect. The gum, which was patented in November 2000 would contain up to 100 milligrams of Sildenil Citrate. But Wrigley has stated it does not intend to produce Viagra flavoured gum at any point in the future, and Pfizer's patent for Viagra has another eight years to run.

90
The percentage by which the price of patented medicines would have to drop for African countries to be able to afford them, according to Dr Jonathan Quick, director of essential drugs and medicines policy at the World Health Organisation. Dr Quick also estimates it would take five different companies providing the same product to bring the price down to an affordable level.

30,000
Number of trademarks the average person encounters in a supermarket during each visit.

Sources: New York Times, The Telegraph, BBC News, Panati's Extraordinary Origin of Everyday Things.

WELL DEFINED

Inventor
A person who makes an ingenious arrangement of wheels, levers and springs, and believes it civilization.

Ambrose Bierce, *The Devil's Dictionary*

ACCIDENTAL INVENTIONS

Saccharin
Back in 1879, Ira Remsen and Constantine Fahlberg were minding their own business, experimenting with coal tar derivatives, as you do. Little did they know that they were about to stumble upon the world's first artificial sweetener. Having spent a day hard at work at John Hopkins University, Remsen decided to have dinner. But he hadn't washed his hands properly and while eating he noticed a sweet residue on his hands. Further tests on what became known as 'saccharin' revealed that it was 300 times as sweet as sucrose and that it could also pass through the body without affecting blood insulin levels, making it an important discovery, especially for diabetics. Realising they were onto a winner, Remsen and Fahlberg published their results in 1880, but Fahlberg decided to go one better and went on to patent the product. Somehow 'forgetting to mention his co-inventor on the patent document, Remsen consequently lost out on any profit to be made from their discovery. Remsen was not one to forgive and forget, remarking that: 'Fahlberg is a scoundrel. It nauseates me to hear my name mentioned in the same breath as him.' It seems that for him saccharin was not so sweet after all.

INTERNATIONAL PATENTS REGISTERED IN 1900, BY NATION

Belgium – 24
Netherlands – 48
France – 165
Italy – 15
Spain – 8
Switzerland – 85

CELEBRITY INVENTORS

Michael Jackson
Michael Jackson is the co-inventor of a 'method and means for creating an anti-gravity illusion'. The secret is a specially designed pair of shoes that attach to the stage, allowing the wearer to 'lean forward beyond his centre of gravity'. The patent was issued in 1993.

This chirpy character was the trademark for a proprietary brand of hair restorer popular in the Midwest during the second decade of the twentieth century. The product promised to turn the purchaser's life completely upside down.

USELESS PATENTS

The 'Alarm Fork'

For those times when you just forget why you have a plate in front of you and a knife and fork in your hands, US patent no. 5,421,089 will sound an alarm to remind you to take another bite of food. It's a god send for absent-minded underfed people.

THE BLACK AND THE WHITE
(AND THE CHUTZPAH)

Stendhal (born Marie Henri Beyle), the great French author of *The Red and the Black*, once wrote a book entitled *The Lives of Haydn, Mozart, and Metastasio* under the pseudonym 'Bombet'. It later emerged that he had 'borrowed' material from two biographies and a eulogy. Far from owning up, Stendhal mounted a vigorous defence of the integrity of the work, writing numerous letters to the press signed 'Bombet Junior'.

ORIGIN OF THE NAME

Frisbee

The name may have a modern ring to it, but even if we ignore the fact that the Ancient Greeks were throwing spinning discs at the Olympics well over two thousand years ago, the Frisbee turns out to have been around for longer than you might think. Back in the late nineteenth century, college students at Yale and other New England universities took to playing catch with pie tins made by the Frisbie Baking Company, based nearby in Bridgeport, Connecticut. To alert their fellows of the imminent risk of decapitation, the students would shout out the name of the product as it sailed through the air. They were still doing this in 1948 when Walter Morrison and Warren Franscioni created a plastic version called the Pluto Platter and started selling it at country fairs. The toy fitted in perfectly with America's growing fascination with UFOs. In 1955, Morrison and Franscioni sold their company to Arthur 'Spud' Melin and Richard Knerr, the inventors of the Hula Hoop. Three years later, the new owners renamed the product the Frisbee in homage to its roots. By the time they sold their Wham-O company to Mattel, sales had exceeded 100 million units.

US PATENTS BY NUMBERS

1,111,111	Device for holding back a horse-drawn vehicle from moving forward (1914)
2,222,222	Folding bed into wall cavity (1940)
3,333,333	Method of making magnetic material with pattern of embedded non-magnetic material (1967)
4,444,444	Equipment for storage of energy under kinetic form and recovery thereof in electric form and method of using such equipment (1984)
5,555,555	Apparatus which detects lines approximating an image by repeatedly narrowing an area of the image to be analysed and increasing the resolution in the analysed area (1996)
6,666,666	Multi-chamber positive displacement fluid device (2003)

IT'S AMAZING NO ONE
THOUGHT OF IT BEFORE

The coffee filter was invented in Germany in 1908. Melissa Bentz simply pierced some holes in a tin container, placed a circular piece of absorbent paper in the bottom and plonked it over a coffee pot.

---

150 *Maximum penalty, in thousands of dollars, for downloading a single copyrighted song in the US*

DURING THE COMPILATION OF THIS BOOK,
THE COMPANION TEAM...

Drank 17 trademarked varieties of vodka

Visited 11,411 websites

Used 37 synonyms for 'plagiarise'

Laughed at 14 Scandinavian brand names

Spent 1.7 hours trying to work out how to
type the ©, ® and ™ symbols and then discarded them altogether

Bought three bottles of fake perfume by mistake at a car boot sale

Wished out loud that 'intellectual property' had a sexier name
54 times

Saw 62,828 images of David Beckham

Convinced 24 friends that it was illegal to sing
'Happy Birthday' in a restaurant.

Thought up 96 witty new domain names

Bought drinks for 27 lawyers

Invented three new excuses for late delivery of copy

*Please note that although every effort has been made to ensure
accuracy in this book, the above statistics may be the result of
brand-addled minds.*

A man better have... anything happen to him in the world, short of losing all his family by influenza, than have a dispute about a patent

Lord Esher

US patent number for an improved method of burning lime 'by the introduction of a blast of air' (1837)

P14   SONY, BONY, BONE, CONE, COKE (There may be others)

P21   Internet piracy

P29   Kerosene (generic), Corn Flakes (generic), Aspirin (ruled generic in US; still a trademark in Canada), Nylon (generic), Transistor (generic – once a trademark)

P35   Telephone. From Alexander Graham Bell's Patent Application for an 'Improvement in Telegraphy', 14 February 1876

P44   (a)-(d); (b)-(c); (c)-(e); (d)-(f); (e)-(b); (f)-(a)

P57   *Because*, from the album *Abbey Road*

P59   (Leonardo) da Vinci. The letters spell 'dav' in 'ci'

P68   Thomas Edison

P81   Trade secrets

P86   (c) Richards and Jagger scored a sweet victory after a bitter legal battle over the extent to which The Verve had sampled the old Stones song *The Last Time*. As a result of the settlement, the Stones achieved the Satisfaction of being granted 100% of the royalties from The Verve's recording

P91   Archimedes

P100   *Yesterday* by the Beatles (McCartney)

P107   Shredded Wheat (generic), escalator (generic according to the Collins English Dictionary, once a trademark), gramophone (generic, once a trademark), linoleum (generic), pyrex (generic)

P120   a2, b5, c6, d4, e1, f3

P122   Tarzan. His yell is a registered trademark, international class 28 (toy action figures), owned by Edgar Rice Burroughs, Inc

P133   Land Rover (Land + 'R' over)

P140   .bn = Brunei, .dj = Djibouti, .ee = Estonia, .fk = Falkland Islands, .ls = Lesotho, .mg = Madagascar, .uy = Uruguay, .tt = Trinidad and Tobago, .va = Vatican City State, .za = South Africa

P146   (Guglielmo) Marconi, radio pioneer. 'Marc' on 'I'

FOR YOUR OWN BRIGHT IDEAS

*The only 'ism' Hollywood believes in
is plagiarism*

Dorothy Parker

ACKNOWLEDGEMENTS

We gratefully acknowledge permission to reprint extracts of copyright material in the book from the following authors, publishers and executors:

'Transcendental Nonsense and the Functional Approach' in *The Columbia Law Review*, 1935 by Felix Cohen reproduced by permission of *Columbia Law Review*.

Reflections on the Human Condition by Eric Hoffer reproduced by permission of HarperCollins.

No Logo © 2000 Naomi Klein, reproduced by permission of HarperCollins. Copyright in the customised version vests in Think Publishing.

No Logo by Naomi Klein reproduced by permission of Westwood Creative Artists and AP Watt Ltd.

White Teeth by Zadie Smith (Hamish Hamilton, 2000). Copyright © Zadie Smith, 2000. Reproduced by permission of Penguin Books Ltd.

White Teeth by Zadie Smith reproduced by permission of The Random House Group Ltd.

The Time Machine by H G Wells reproduced by permission of AP Watt Ltd on behalf of The Literary Executors of the Estate of H G Wells.

INDEX

FILL YOUR BOOKSHELF AND YOUR MIND

The Birdwatcher's Companion Twitchers, birders, ornithologists and garden-tickers: there are many species of birdwatcher, and you're all catered for by this unique book. ISBN 1-86105-833-0

The Cook's Companion Whether your taste is for foie gras or fry-ups, this tasty compilation is an essential ingredient in any kitchen, boiling over with foodie fact and fiction. ISBN 1-86105-772-5

The Gardener's Companion For anyone who has ever put on a pair of gloves, picked up a spade and gone out into the garden in search of flowers, beauty and inspiration. ISBN 1-86105-771-7

The Golfer's Companion Bogeys and shanking, plus fours and six irons, the alleged etiquette of caddies – all you need to know about the heaven and hell of golf is in this unique book. ISBN 1-86105-834-9

The Ideas Companion This fascinating book tells the stories behind the trademarks, inventions, and brands that we come across every day. ISBN 1-86105-835-7

The Legal Companion From lawmakers to lawbreakers, this fascinating compilation offers a view of the oddities, quirks, origins and stories behind the legal world. ISBN 1-86105-838-1

The Literary Companion Whether your Dickens is Charles or Monica, your Stein Gertrude or Franken, here's your book. Literary fact and fiction from Rebecca East to Vita Sackville-West. ISBN 1-86105-798-9

The London Companion From Edgware to Morden, Upminster to Ealing, here's your chance to explore the history and mystery of the most exciting capital city in the world. ISBN 1-86105-799-7

The Moviegoer's Companion Explore the strange and wonderful world of movies, actors, cinemas and salty popcorn in all their glamorous glory from film noir to Matt LeBlanc. ISBN 1-86105-797-0

The Politics Companion The history, myths, great leaders and greater liars of international politics are all gathered around the hustings in this remarkable compilation. ISBN 1-86105-796-2

The Sailing Companion This is the book for everyone who knows their starboard from their stinkpot, and their Raggie from their stern – and anybody who wants to find out. ISBN 1-86105-839-X

The Traveller's Companion For anyone who's ever stared at a distant plane, wondered where it's going, and spent the rest of the day dreaming of faraway lands. ISBN 1-86105-773-3

The Walker's Companion If you've ever laced a sturdy boot, packed a cheese sandwich, and stepped out in search of stimulation and contemplation, then this book is for you. ISBN 1-86105-825-X

The Wildlife Companion Animal amazements, ornithological oddities and botanical beauties abound in this compilation of natural need-to-knows and nonsense for wildlife-lovers. ISBN 1-86105-770-9